N Scale
Model Railroading

Getting Started in the Hobby

Marty McGuirk

KALMBACH
BOOKS

Printed in the United States of America

04 05 06 07 08   10 9 8 7 6 5 4 3

Visit our website at
http://kalmbachbooks.com
Secure online ordering available

Publisher's Cataloging in Publication
(Provided by Quality Books, Inc.)

McGuirk, Martin J.
    N scale model railroading / Marty McGuirk. —
1st ed.
    p. cm.
    Includes index.
    ISBN 0-89024-347-6

    1. Railroads—Models. I. Title

  TF197.M34 1999   625.1'9
                                QBI99-580

Book design: Mark Watson
Cover design: Kristi Ludwig

Photography by Marty McGuirk unless otherwise noted

Some of the material in this book has previously appeared as articles in *Model Railroader* magazine. They are reprinted in their entirety and may include an occasional reference to an item elsewhere in the same issue or in a previous issue.

CONTENTS

CHAPTER ONE

THIS IS N SCALE

The purpose of this book is to help you get started by showing you everything you need to know to build and operate your very own N scale empire. In writing this book I've tried to answer all the questions I had when I got started in the hobby. I've included some general tips as well as some specific how-to projects. I hope it answers many, if not all, of your questions.

What is N scale?

If you've flipped through this book or leafed through an issue of *Model Railroader* magazine, you've already discovered that there is always something new to learn in the hobby. My advice is to digest it slowly. The terminology used in model railroading is one of the toughest things for beginners, but don't try to memorize everything all at once. You may not know the difference between a PS-1 and a GP7 today, but with time you'll be talking like an old hand. One of the first lessons is the most basic—the difference between scale and gauge. Scale is simply the proportion of a model in relationship to the real thing. N scale is built to a ratio of 1:160. That is, N scale trains are ¹⁄₁₆₀ the size of the real thing (fig. 1-1). The same rule holds true for buildings, automobiles, figures, trees, roads—everything. Figure 1-2 shows some significant N scale dimensions.

Technically, the word "gauge" refers to the distance between the rails. In the United States, Canada, and most of Europe, trains run on tracks with the rails spaced 4'8½" apart. This is referred to as "standard gauge."

Years ago many prototype railroads ("prototype" is what model railroaders call the real thing) were built with narrower track gauges. Three-foot was the most common in the U. S., although a few railroads in Maine had two-foot track gauge. Model railroaders refer to these narrow gauge railroads using the scale followed by the small letter "n" (for narrow) and the track gauge in feet. So HOn3 means HO scale (1:87 proportion), 3-scale-foot gauge. Some advanced N scalers even build Nn3 layouts. To avoid confusion, throughout this book I'll use the term "N scale" to refer to 1:160 proportion model trains that are designed to run on N scale standard gauge track.

Perhaps it would help you to understand N scale if I placed it in relation to the other modeling scales. According to the latest *Model Railroader* magazine survey, N scale is currently the second-most-popular modeling scale in the United States. While most active N scalers consider N scale to be their primary modeling scale, some model in another scale and consider N scale to be a secondary interest.

The Wisconsin Central is an aggressive and successful regional railroad, making it a perfect prototype for an N scale layout. A group of N scale modelers from Madison, Wisconsin, built this N scale version of the WC as a project layout for *Model Railroader* magazine. The SD45s are Kato models. Jeff Wilson

Fig. 1-1 **N scale trains are fascinating miniature machines that are precise duplicates of the real thing. Shown here are an N scale SD40 and the prototype locomotive on which it was based.**

As I mentioned earlier, N scale is 1:160 proportion. Two other popular model railroad scales are 1:87 proportion, called HO (pronounced "Aitch-Oh"), and O scale, which is 1:48 proportion. For many years HO has been the dominant scale, and the sheer numbers mean that it has the greatest selection of locomotives, rolling stock, and accessories. O scale was the leading scale in the formative years of the hobby, and despite a recent resurgence in new products, still remains far behind HO and N. Also included are S and G, or large scales. All are shown side by side in fig. 1-3.

So if HO is the top dog, why bother with N scale? The primary, and most obvious reason, is that N scale takes up so much less space than HO. N scale models are 54.5 percent the size of equivalent HO models. This means you can build an N scale layout in an area about 30 percent the size of a comparable HO layout. Most starter HO layouts are built on the traditional 4 x 8 sheet of plywood. With N scale you can pack all the same action onto a small interior door and have room to spare! Later in this book, I'll show you how to build an N scale layout on such a door—one that'll knock your HO modeling buddies' socks off!

But there's another significant advantage to building in N scale, even if you have enough space for an HO layout. The real world is a big place, and every time we model railroaders try to cram even a small part of it into even the largest room we have to compromise. Towns that are supposedly miles apart are separated by a few feet, and we wish our 25-car trains were more like the prototype's 100-car trains.

If you truly want to capture the look of mainline railroading, I suggest taking an area large enough for a medium HO scale layout and building that layout in N scale. More and more HO modelers are growing dissatisfied with the limitations of what will fit in the space they have available and are turning to N scale. Suddenly those sharp HO curves look broad and majestic as a long train of beautifully detailed N scale cars roll past. And speaking of N scale trains, don't let anyone ever tell you N scale "doesn't operate." Anyone who holds that opinion hasn't seen the better N scale equipment on the market today. True enough, in N scale's early, dark beginnings,

there were many teething problems. Wheel flanges were too large and locomotives either ran too fast or, in some cases, didn't work at all. Today's N scale equipment is the equivalent of that found in any scale.

Ways to enjoy N scale railroading

There are as many ways to enjoy a hobby as there are participants. The only "rule" (and it's not really a rule, it's just common sense!) is to have fun and enjoy it.

While one person will find building models and then developing a layout to be an ideal way to spend his or her hobby time, another person may find a club setting—either a traditional club with a permanent layout or an Ntrak club—to be the most rewarding way to enjoy the hobby and spend time with other modelers at the same time.

Among the most common ways to enjoy N scale model railroading are building a home layout, building an Ntrak module, building models of locomotives, cars, and buildings, and collecting some of the beautifully detailed N scale models that have been made. Rather than concentrate on just one aspect of the hobby, most N scalers combine some or all of these activities. Some N scalers even find that collecting is a legitimate way to participate in the hobby. However, for this book I'll concentrate on building and modeling.

Perhaps the main goal of all beginning model railroaders is to build a realistic and functional layout. In a sense, model railroading is a combination of several hobbies and skills, brought together for the ultimate goal of creating a complete layout.

Before you jump headlong into building that first layout, be sure to avoid the three biggest pitfalls that cause beginners (and some advanced modelers) the most trouble:
1. Trying to do too much at first
2. Refusing to try new materials or techniques
3. Failing to correct mistakes

The solution to problem no. 1 is easy: Start small. Make your first layout small and simple, but complete it. Building an Ntrak module is an ideal way to cut your teeth, and if you have a club nearby you'll find the members are a great source of inspiration and camaraderie. Follow the entire

Prototype dimension in inches	N scale equivalent dimension in inches	Prototype dimension in inches/feet	N scale equivalent dimension in inches
¹⁄₆₄	.0001	4¼	.02656
¹⁄₃₂	.00019	4½	.02812
¹⁄₁₆	.00039	5	.03125
⅛	.00078	5¼	.03281
¼	.00156	5½	.03437
⅜	.00234	6	.0375
½	.00312	6¼	.03906
⅝	.0039	6½	.04062
¾	.00468	7	.04375
⅞	.00546	8	.05
1	.00625	9	.05625
1⅛	.00703	10	.0625
1¼	.00781	11	.06875
1⅜	.00859		
1½	.00937		
1⅝	.01015	1'	.075
1¾	.01093	2'	.15
1⅞	.01171	3'	.225
2	.0125	4'	.30
2¼	.01406	5'	.375
2½	.01562	6'	.45
3	.01875	7'	.525
3¼	.02031	8'	.60
3½	.02187	9'	.675
4	.025	10'	.75

Here's an example of how to use this table. Find the N scale equivalent of 5'6¹⁵⁄₁₆".

Prototype	5'0"	=	.375" in N scale
	6"	=	.0375"
	⅞"	=	.00546"
	¹⁄₁₆"	=	.00039"
	5'6¹⁵⁄₁₆"	=	.41835"

Fig. 1-2 N SCALE CONVERSION TABLE

sequence of construction up to and including scenery and detailing. This will give you a chance to get a feel for every step of construction without getting bogged down in any one phase. With a small layout you'll often find that just about the time you get tired of one part of the process it's time to move on to the next.

When you start feeling comfortable with your abilities using one set of techniques, it's time to move on to step 2: Try different techniques. That may seem to be a contradiction. After all, once you get good at something, why would you want to

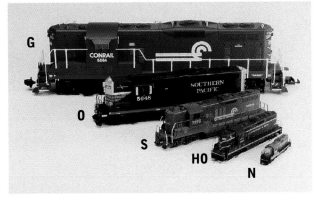

Fig. 1-3 **Popular modeling scales. All these locomotives are models of the popular EMD GP9. Shown from right to left are N, HO, S, O, and large (often called G) scale models.**

change? Simple. As time goes on you'll be reading model railroad magazines and books and finding all sorts of interesting techniques from other hobbyists like yourself. Try them! If some new method of doing something doesn't work for you, it's no big deal. But if they do work, you may surprise yourself and find the results better than you imagined.

And finally, through the whole process of building not only your first, but every model railroad, don't be afraid to correct mistakes. Sure, the train makes it around that curve about half the time, so why fix it? Believe me, take the time to fix it and you'll be much happier in the long run. Not happy with the way the mountain looks? Rip it out and start afresh. There's no time clock running on getting this layout built. And when it's in the final phases of detailing (which can go on indefinitely) you'll be secure in the knowledge that it works as it should and looks as good as it can.

Throughout this book you'll find various tips and techniques that I've tried and used with success in my own modeling. There is a veritable gold mine of information available to modelers today. Kalmbach Publishing offers how-to books that go into far more detail on every aspect of the hobby. Also, *Model Railroader* magazine, published by Kalmbach, is the oldest and largest magazine in the world devoted exclusively to scale model railroading. Since close to 20 percent of MR's readers are N scalers, you'll always find an article or two specific to N scale in every issue. Also, the ideas and techniques in every article can be adapted for N scale layouts and models.

Most of this book is devoted to helping you grow from your first N scale train set to your first N scale layout. By the time you've built that first layout you'll find you've learned new skills, overcome challenges, discovered you have talent for one or more specific aspects of the hobby, and, best of all, had some fun in the process.

CHAPTER TWO

PLANNING YOUR RAILROAD

While there's no "right" or "wrong" way to design a model railroad, no other process, except perhaps anxiously awaiting the release of a new locomotive model, causes so many model railroaders to loose sleep—or offers so much grist for the local bull session. If you don't believe me, take your track plan down to the club or hobby shop. Minutes after you present the plan everyone will look it over, and many of them will offer advice. Be sure to listen and take notes, as their comments may be just what you're looking for.

Prototype, free-lance, or somewhere in between?

You don't have to be involved in model railroading for long before someone will ask what you model. There are any number of answers to that question, of course, but the answer will typically come in one of three categories: You're a prototype modeler, a free-lancer, or something in the middle. The lines of division aren't clear cut, and absolutes are never completely true. In fact, every good layout I can think of incorporates elements of at least two—and in many cases, all three. But for purposes of discussion, here's a rough overview of each of these approaches. Which you fall into will tell you a lot about what kind of layout you will want to design.

Fig. 2-1 **N scale layouts don't have to be small coffee table affairs. If you have the space N scale allows you to capture scenic vistas. Lyn St. Laurent's circa 1949 Southern Pacific layout featured this impressive version of Tehachapi Loop, a famous real location in Southern California.** Keith Thompson

Fig. 2-2 Mike Hurlburt chose a southern New England setting for his free-lanced N scale Trap & Garnet Ridge. The T&GR interchanges with a prototype railroad, Conrail, which helps place the free-lanced line in the real world. Keith Thompson

Prototype. In a way, all model railroaders model prototype, or real railroading, to some degree. This term has come to mean those who model a specific railroad or railroads as faithfully as possible. This includes not only the trains, but the buildings, bridges, towns, and even the recognizable scenic features of a specific place.

Prototype modelers choose a specific time period to model as well, and research everything about that era in detail. With the explosion in product availability, and the chance to model expansive scenery, N scale prototype modeling has grown in popularity in recent years. Other advantages of prototype modeling include:

Focus. Selecting a prototype railroad and an era and sticking to it provide the focus some model railroaders need if they're ever to get a layout built. With a clearly defined focus, it's easier to stay on track and get things done without getting distracted by every new car and locomotive that comes along.

More economical. Prototype modeling can be less expensive than other approaches. If a new locomotive, structure kit, or car isn't appropriate for your chosen prototype and era you can pass it up, saving valuable hobby dollars for something that is appropriate.

More challenging. It's easy to compromise on the side of convenience when you free-lance, but prototype modelers really don't have that luxury. The result is more work, but the results can be much more satisfying.

Easier layout design. Prototype layouts are, by definition, easier to plan. After all, the real world is already there. All we have to do is figure out a way to model it.

Free-lancing. I fall kinda hard on the prototype side of the model railroading fence, but I still appreciate modeling that doesn't closely follow a prototype railroad. If you like to buy anything in the shop you happen to see, or even if you just like to watch the trains run around continuously, there are plenty of ways that you can enjoy this hobby too!

Prototype free-lancing. There is a middle-of-the-road approach, which combines the best of both prototype modeling and pure, unadulterated free-lancing. This approach, which was called "prototype free-lancing" by well-known model railroad author Tony Koester, simply means taking the best of both worlds. You can invent your own railroad and set it in a real area of the country. That's perhaps the most common type of prototype free-lancing. Maybe your favorite railroad didn't run through the mountains, but you just love to watch long trains of hoppers snake through the hills. Add a free-lanced extension to your favorite prototype, and maybe even give it its own name. Another form of prototype free-lancing is not quite so obvious, but it's still a tremendous time and effort saver. For instance, at the town of Essex Junction on my home layout, I scratchbuilt a rather

Fig. 2-3 What are the signature elements, items that must be modeled to capture the flavor of this prototype photo? The photo shows Essex Junction, Vermont, on the Central Vermont Railway. Jim Shaughnessy

Fig. 2-4 Here's the author's model of Essex Junction. It features a scratchbuilt model of the trainshed, a significant signature item that needed the extra effort. The other structures are kits that he painted and weathered to resemble the prototype structures with very little effort.

elaborate model of the unique covered trainshed that once stood in town. But when I started counting the number of buildings, all of which would be scratchbuilt if the layout was to be a "true" prototype model of the real place, I knew I'd never get them all built in a lifetime. For that reason I resorted to using some modified N scale kits and scratchbuilt structures

The layout plan

If you thought I meant to say "track plan," you're wrong. While a track plan is an important component of any layout design, it's only one part of a several-step process.

This process has served me well in helping other modelers design layouts, as well as designing layouts for *Model Railroader* magazine. I've also used the same process to design layouts ranging from shelf switching layouts and layouts designed to be built on a door all the way to my present basement-sized home layout. Every time I've used this process the result has been a workable layout plan that's practical to build and has a viable theme. Here are the steps you'll want to follow:

• **Pick a prototype railroad (or railroads) that you're interested in.** Ask yourself, "Where is this railroad supposedly located and what does it do for a living? Answers to those two questions will be invaluable when it comes time to draw track plans. This is also a good time to start narrowing down the era you're most interested in. It's okay to keep the time period fairly broad at this stage with the understanding that you'll narrow the focus as you go along.

• **Determine what you find appealing about your chosen prototype.** You're looking for "signature items"—those things that make the railroad you've chosen recognizable. Keep this list fairly broad. Try to list at least one thing for each of the following categories: traffic, locomotives, rolling stock, right-of-way, railroad structures, industries, town structures, and scenery. Stay away from the unique and unusual. The idea is to capture the

OVERPASS LOOP GRADES		
	GRADE	
Radius	($1^5/_8$") Minimum separation	(2") Normal separation
8"	3.0%	3.7%
9"	2.7%	3.3%
10"	2.4%	3.0%
11"	2.2%	2.7%
12"	2.0%	2.5%
14"	1.7%	2.1%
16"	1.5%	1.9%
18"	1.4%	1.7%

KEY PLANNING DATA	
Proportion from prototype	1/160
Scale foot in actual inches	.075"=1 foot
Standard track gauge	.354"
Minimum track radius	$7^1/_2$"
Minimum track center-to-center separation	$1^1/_4$"
Separation of tracks at overhead crossings	2"
Clearance from top of rail to underside of bridge or structure	$1^5/_8$"
Clearance from center of straight track to structures at side	$5/_8$"

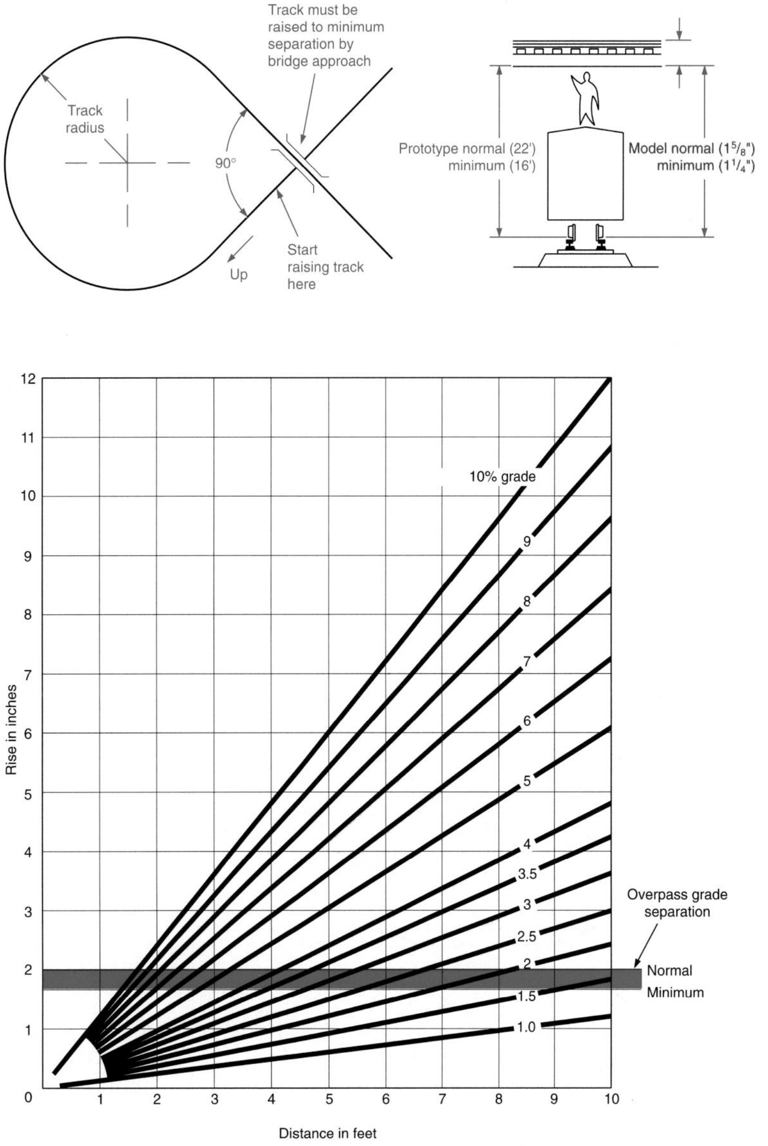

Fig. 2-5 **Key planning data**

essence of the prototype. You can make a few mental notes, but I prefer to actually list the signature items on paper.

Then make a second list, this one showing everything you'd include on a layout based on your chosen prototype. Again, the same rules

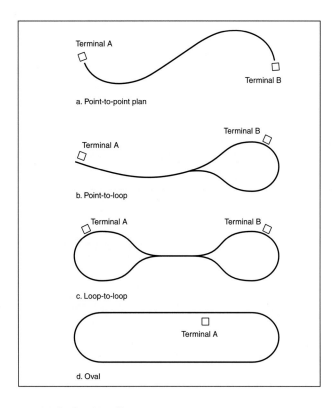

Fig. 2-6 **Basic schematics**

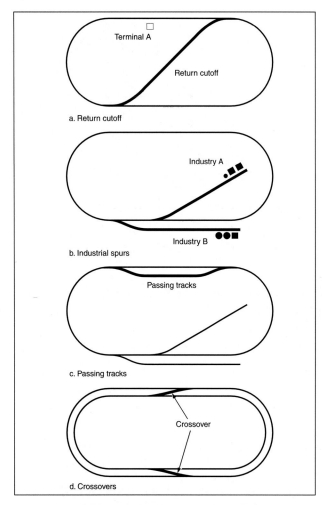

Fig. 2-7 **Variations on the basic oval**

apply for free-lanced approaches. Prioritize this list, and then take the bottom half and throw it out. Compare this "dream" list with the list of signature items from the previous paragraph. Get rid of any dream items that do not match up with the signature items.

Is that all there is to it? No. Happily, the world isn't so cut and dried. Let's say your signature item list shows "steel mills." But you find one of the railroad's coal branches to be far more interesting, even though the road is not typically thought of as a mountain branchline railroad. It's obvious that some common sense and a little modeler's license is called for throughout this process. You may also find that some additional research is required.

Let's review where we are in this process. We have a prototype railroad and a rough idea of the time period and geographic locale we're interested in. We've also got a list of common elements that will capture the essence of that railroad. It's time to stop the dream stage and get down to reality. Let's see how practical this would be.

• **Assess practical factors.** All model railroaders are limited by practical factors. The most obvious is the availability of appropriate commercial models for the railroad you're planning. If no model is available, you may want to consider changing the time period you plan to model or even selecting a new prototype. A third choice would be to create a free-lanced subsidiary of that prototype railroad that you imagine ran locomotives that are available in N scale.

Take a long, hard look at each of these factors. Also, as we will see when we discuss locomotives in Chapter Six, there are many more reliable diesel models than steam locomotives available to choose from. The ease of maintaining diesel locomotives makes them my first choice.

Three other practical factors that aren't so specific to any particular railroad are perhaps the most important to address early on: time, space, skill level, and money. If you have a great deal of disposable income and little spare time, you'll want to choose a theme for your railroad that lets you use a lot of prepainted and ready-to-run equipment. If, on the other hand, you don't have a great deal of cash, but you have good modeling skills, you can make up for the lack of disposable income by scratchbuilding and custom-painting. This is a hobby, not a race, but you're much more likely to be satisfied with the end result if you know what you're getting into early on. By the same token, if you have a large basement, but have never built a layout before, build only a small starter layout at first. This will keep your interest high and help you gain the skill level necessary to tackle an elaborate layout with confidence.

Finally, even the best plan isn't worth the paper it's drawn on if the trains won't work. Keep the grades reasonable and the curves workable. Figure 2-5 contains lots of key planning data on minimum radius, grades, curves, and clearances.

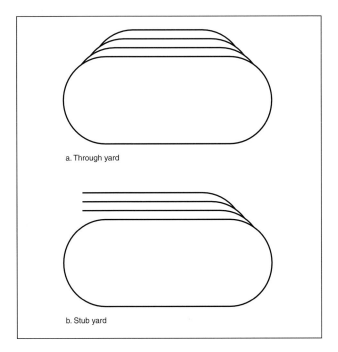

Fig. 2-8 **Yards**

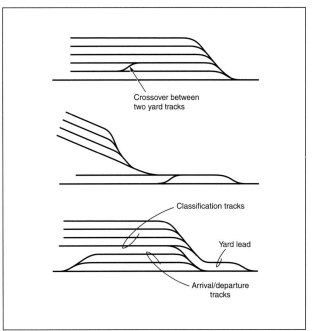

Crossover between
two yard tracks

Classification tracks

Yard lead

Arrival/departure
tracks

Fig. 2-9 **Anatomy of a basic yard**

Fig. 2-10 **Bill Denton was inspired by an April 1975** *Model Rail-roader* **story to model the Kingsbury branch. This shot shows some of the area he's captured on his layout.**

Fig. 2-11 **Bill's Kingsbury branch is not only an example of out-standing modeling, it's also an operator's delight. The buildings really dominate the trains running through the "brick canyons."**
Bill Denton

• **Draw the plan.** Make a detailed measure-ment of available space. Be sure to include all the obvious obstructions such as doors, walls, and windows and other items that may get in the way when it comes time to build the layout. These include appliances, pipes, furnaces, hot water heaters, ductwork, and the like. It's possible to design a layout to work its way around many of these obstructions, but remember you need to keep them accessible for possible future repairs and replacement.

Track planning

Although many computer layout design programs are available, I find my favorite layout designing tools are an architect's scale ruler, some graph paper, a few sharp pencils, and an N scale track template. I also keep a compass handy for drawing curves.

When you get to track-planning, you have the choice of using a published plan or designing your own from scratch. You can also "planbash"—that is, combine elements from one or more plans to develop a pleasing arrangement. Whichever approach you choose, there are a few track planning fundamentals you should be familiar with.

Basic schematics. Prototype trains run from one place to another and back again, stopping at stations in between. A model railroad arranged in this manner is a point-to-point system. See fig. 2-6a. Adding a return loop to one end of the point-to-point system makes it a point-to-loop design (fig. 2-6b).

A loop at both ends of the original point-to-point creates a loop-to-loop system (fig. 2-6c). Finally, connecting the two ends of the original loop-to-loop together creates an oval or circle (fig. 2-6d).

Oval and loop-to-loop schematics provide for nonstop operation of trains. This can make the main line seem longer, since you can run the train around several times to represent mainline mileage before stopping it to perform work. The other schematics require stopping the train at one or both ends of the line to run the locomotive around the train, or in the case of a steam locomotive, to turn it around. You can vary the oval schematic slightly by adding a return cutoff from one side of the oval to another as shown in fig. 2-7a. The train can be turned on this track so it comes back to the station from a different direction.

It's important to remember: no matter how many places the track goes, and no matter how big or small the layout is, all model railroads are based on a schematic. Some of the more complicated layouts may combine elements of one or more schematics, but the schematic is still the heart of the track plan. In addition to the schematic you'll also want to consider other tracks to add operating interest and provide a place to store trains when they aren't actually running on the line.

Industrial spurs are a great way to improve even the simplest plan. A typical spur is shown in fig. 2-7b. Many published plans show industrial spurs, but you may want to add additional spurs or rearrange them so your favorite industries will fit

PLANNING THE SCENERY

Let's take a moment to consider what kind of scenery to build. Obviously, a layout based on the Rocky Mountains of Colorado will look a great deal different than one showing the Southern Pacific running along the ocean. Likewise, a layout set in the city will have scenery much different from one showing the open countryside.

Many modelers run into trouble when they plan and build a layout without considering scenic elements. But planning for scenery should occur along with layout design. Even the largest layouts are too small to allow for full scale scenic effects, but luckily it's fairly easy to compress scenery so that it looks good even on a small layout. Your goal in building scenery is to suggest the terrain modeled without trying to depict every hill, outcropping, and bush.

Design significant scenic elements as you're planning the layout. That way, when it comes time to build them, you'll know there'll be enough room for everything. Be sure to plan for larger scenic features such as

mountains, roads, waterways, towns and cities, or any larger structures.

You also need to keep the prototype in mind when planning your scenic treatment. Mountain railroads often follow river courses, meaning that the mountains will tower above the tracks. On the plains, railroads don't have to contend with steep mountain grades, but they have to cross rivers by passing over fairly deep ravines. Also consider the shape of the hills and the degree of slope. The Rockies feature much steeper slopes than the eastern Appalachians, which have been worn down by Mother Nature for a much longer time.

I find most model railroads feature terrain that's too steep. When in doubt, make the slopes gentle and keep the hilltops to a reasonable height. Finally, be sure to include some scenery below track level, such as a river or a dry wash. Not only does this add interest to the layout, it also does wonders for getting rid of the "Ping-Pong table" look—a common problem in which layouts look as though the track has been plopped down on the ground.

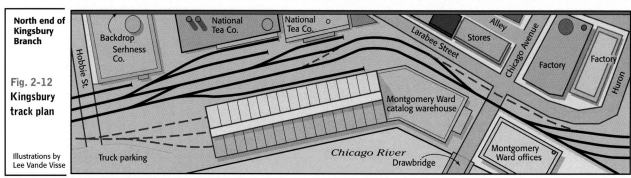

North end of Kingsbury Branch

Fig. 2-12 **Kingsbury track plan**

Illustrations by Lee Vande Visse

Hobbie St.

Backdrop Serhness Co.

National Tea Co.

National Tea Co.

Larabee Street

Stores

Alley

Chicago Avenue

Factory

Factory

Huron

Montgomery Ward catalog warehouse

Truck parking

Chicago River

Drawbridge

Montgomery Ward offices

What does "staging" mean, you ask? As the name implies, staging tracks are tracks that represent "backstage" or "everywhere else." They can take any form—the rear half of an oval, as on the Carolina Central (see Chapters 11 and 12), a through hidden yard, a stub-ended or loop yard, or even a single track that disappears behind the trees or a hill. Staging tracks can be out in the open in the same room as the layout, hidden under the scenery, or accessed by a track running through a wall into an adjacent area. What form staging takes is less important than what staging tracks do. Simply put, they open up the operating potential of even the simplest layout.

Imagine this—instead of running a train around the main line you run a train out of the staging yard representing Los Angeles, onto the scenicked portion of the layout where you can meet another train, drop off or pick up some cars in the yard, and even work a few local industries. Then your train leaves the visible portion of the layout and heads for Chicago. In reality it could be heading back onto the same track it started on, but with a little imagination you've managed to re-create a small amount of the drama and majesty of big-time railroading. All this at the expense of a few pieces of track and some turnouts! Staging is truly the biggest bargain in the model railroading hobby.

better. If you can back the locomotive into the spur and run it out again, then it's called a trailing-point spur. If heading into the spur means the engine will be trapped in the siding by its own train, then it's said to be a facing-point spur. Note that the name used for the spur is based on the direction of travel, not the actual track arrangement.

Passing tracks. If you want to run more than one train at a time, as most modelers do, you'll have to build a double-track railroad or find some way for trains to pass each other. You do this by adding passing sidings as shown in fig. 2-7c. Plan to include as many passing sidings as possible. The standard rule is one siding in each town, where the passing siding can also serve as a runaround track for switching facing-point spurs.

Crossovers. If you have a double-track main line, the trains going in opposite directions need never meet one another. But adding a pair of crossovers between the two tracks will allow a fast train to overtake a slower train traveling in the same direction. Pull one of the two trains into the "wrong" main to let the other one past, then return the first train to the "correct" main. See fig. 2-7d.

Yard tracks. A prototype yard is composed of many smaller yards, each of which serves a particular function. But most yards are either stub or through yards, as shown in fig. 2-8. The stub yard is often used because it's cheaper to build and maintain. A stub yard also holds more cars than a through yard in the same space, since less space is required for turnouts in the stub facility. Fig. 2-9

shows the makeup of a typical small yard. In this case the arrival and departure tracks are double-ended, allowing the yardmaster to use those tracks for trains going in either direction, depending on traffic. The classification tracks are the tracks on which trains are made up and broken down. They are stub-ended.

Additional track-planning tips

It's impossible to literally scale down a prototype facility and model it foot for foot. As I said, the major goal is to look for interesting features and then incorporate them into the plan. Perhaps you'll find there is an interesting station, freight house, or coal mine that you just have to model. Can you duplicate it on the layout? Look over the prototype track arrangement and see if there's anything that would make an interesting focal point for your layout.

A perfect example of a model railroader who wanted to capture the spirit of a prototype railroad is Bill Denton. Bill was inspired by a *Model Railroader* "Railroad You Can Model" story on a Milwaukee Road branch that served a number of industries in an older section of Chicago. He particularly liked the street trackage and way the buildings created brick canyons for the railroad to run through, under, and around (fig. 2-10). The resulting point-to-point layout (figs. 2-11 and 2-12) is not only an example of exceptional modeling, it speaks volumes for the potential of N scale for prototype modelers.

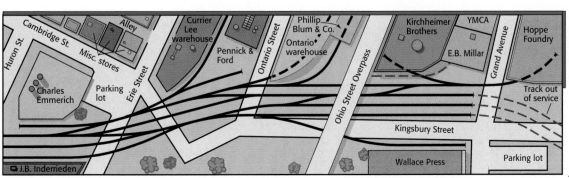

CHAPTER THREE

BENCHWORK

Building a Firm Foundation

Since N scale trains are so small and light, you might think you don't need to bother with a sturdy foundation. But no matter where you build your layout, you need to construct a stable, rigid supporting structure—what model railroaders call "benchwork." Benchwork provides a firm surface for securing the subroadbed, roadbed, and track, as well as a place to mount the scenery.

But what if you want a layout that's fairly lightweight? Suppose you want to put it away, so you can use the room for other purposes? Or take the layout to shows, so other modelers can see it? In those cases, a solid plywood table is hardly the best solution. Luckily, there are other ways to build benchwork that make it easy to allow changes in elevation, variations in the scenery, and, if it's a priority, lightweight construction. A number of layouts have even been built without using any wood at all!

Benchwork is composed of several parts. Since we will be referring to these parts shortly, a few definitions are in order. The framework provides a solid mounting surface for the subroadbed. The framework can be either open-frame or solid-top. In some cases, you'll find it advantageous to combine both of these in one layout. For example, where there are large numbers of tracks or structures, you'll want to have a large, flat area. But when the track runs through the open coun-

tryside you'll find the open-frame method of framework construction more advantageous. The subroadbed is the wood supporting structure for the track roadbed.

The most common methods of constructing model railroad benchwork are solid-top, cookie-cutter, open-frame, and Styrofoam (fig. 3-1).

Let's look at each of these briefly. For a more detailed explanation of constructing model railroad benchwork, you'll want to read *How to Build Model Railroad Benchwork* from Kalmbach Publishing Co.

Solid-top. Solid-top construction offers several advantages. First, it requires the least amount of carpentry work. Ready-to-assemble workbench legs are available at many home improvement centers, eliminating the need to construct legs. In this method, the entire layout is built on a sheet of solid material, typically plywood, although a piece of rigid Styrofoam can be used. (Use the solid type sold for building insulation, not the white bead-board material like that used in coolers.) The track components can be laid out full-size on the table, so you know everything fits. It's also easy to make changes to the track plan before proceeding. The problem with a solid-top layout becomes quickly apparent when you try to add scenery below the track or have the track climb up and over itself. Modifications and repairs are difficult because everything must be done from the top.

Benchwork is foundation of your entire layout. Make it a solid one.

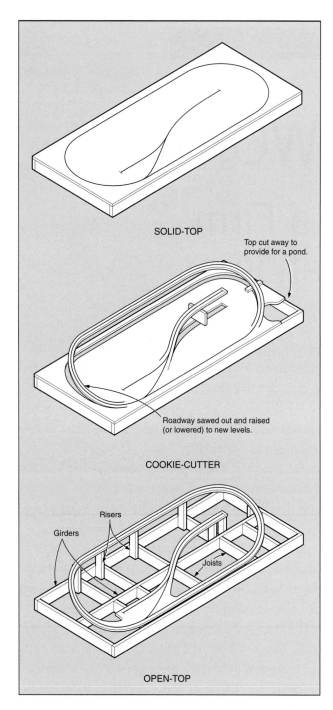

SOLID-TOP

Top cut away to provide for a pond.

Roadway sawed out and raised (or lowered) to new levels.

COOKIE-CUTTER

Girders

Risers

Joists

OPEN-TOP

Fig. 3-1 Table-top benchwork

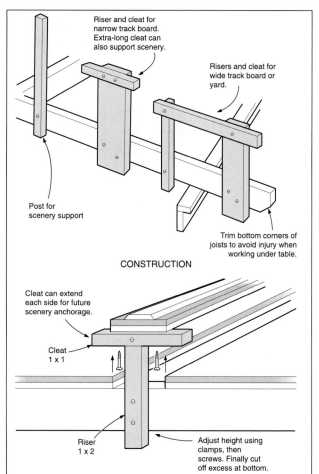

Riser and cleat for narrow track board. Extra-long cleat can also support scenery.

Risers and cleat for wide track board or yard.

Post for scenery support

Trim bottom corners of joists to avoid injury when working under table.

CONSTRUCTION

Cleat can extend each side for future scenery anchorage.

Cleat 1 x 1

Riser 1 x 2

Adjust height using clamps, then screws. Finally cut off excess at bottom.

Fig. 3-2 Installation

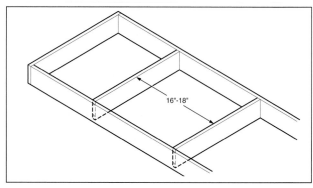

16"-18"

Fig. 3-3 Open-grid benchwork

Cookie-cutter. This improvement over the solid-top method makes it possible to raise and lower the track easily. Initially, building a cookie-cutter benchwork is the same as solid-top. Place the top onto the supporting frame and lay out the track. Then mark the areas where you want scenery below track level and draw lines along both sides of the track where the track will be raised or lowered. Then use a saber saw to cut away the plywood and install risers on the framework to support the plywood at the desired height.

Open-grid. As the name implies, with this method the top of the layout is left open. The only solid surface is the subroadbed, which is cut to fit directly below the track level. The subroadbed is supported above the framework using short vertical pieces called risers. See fig. 3-2.

Once the risers are fastened in place, subroadbed is added. This can be constructed in several ways. Most modelers use a saber saw to cut plywood to the shape of the track. (Plywood ½" thick is okay, but many modelers prefer ¾".) Another technique, called spline-lattice subroadbed, uses two or three edge-mounted wood strips shaped to match the curves. This method is suited for larger layouts with curves of 18" radius or greater because bending the wood strips to form sharper curves is difficult. It also

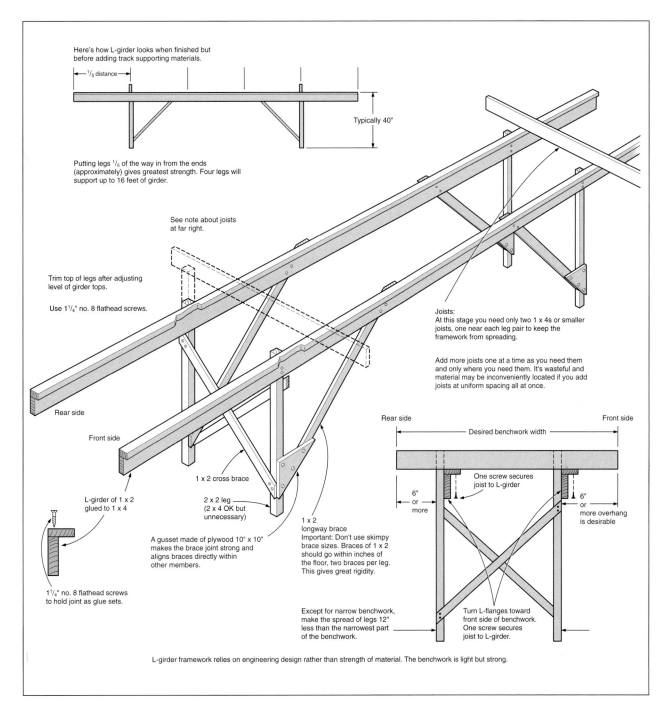

Here's how L-girder looks when finished but before adding track supporting materials.

1/5 distance

Typically 40"

Putting legs 1/5 of the way in from the ends (approximately) gives greatest strength. Four legs will support up to 16 feet of girder.

See note about joists at far right.

Trim top of legs after adjusting level of girder tops.

Use 1 1/4" no. 8 flathead screws.

Rear side

Front side

L-girder of 1 x 2 glued to 1 x 4

1 1/4" no. 8 flathead screws to hold joint as glue sets.

1 x 2 cross brace

2 x 2 leg (2 x 4 OK but unnecessary)

A gusset made of plywood 10" x 10" makes the brace joint strong and aligns braces directly within other members.

1 x 2 longway brace Important: Don't use skimpy brace sizes. Braces of 1 x 2 should go within inches of the floor, two braces per leg. This gives great rigidity.

Joists: At this stage you need only two 1 x 4s or smaller joists, one near each leg pair to keep the framework from spreading.

Add more joists one at a time as you need them and only where you need them. It's wasteful and material may be inconveniently located if you add joists at uniform spacing all at once.

Rear side   Front side

Desired benchwork width

One screw secures joist to L-girder

6" or more

6" or more overhang is desirable

Except for narrow benchwork, make the spread of legs 12" less than the narrowest part of the benchwork.

Turn L-flanges toward front side of benchwork. One screw secures joist to L-girder.

L-girder framework relies on engineering design rather than strength of material. The benchwork is light but strong.

Fig. 3-4 **L-girder benchwork**

requires more cutting than other methods, but modelers who use it prefer the natural easements that result.

Framework construction

The two most common methods of building model railroad framing are butt-joint, usually called "open-grid," and L-girder.

Open-grid. This type of benchwork consists of girders of 1 x 2 lumber or larger (1 x 4 is most common), which run along the edges of the layout area, and crosspieces, called joists, which reach from side to side and across the ends. For an illustration of this type of benchwork, see fig. 3-3.

The biggest disadvantage of this method is the need for accurate cuts to produce solid joints at the ends of the individual pieces.

L-girder. This method of framing was developed by Linn Westcott, the late editor of *Model Railroader*. L-girder derives its name from the shape of the main girders, which are inverted Ls. See fig 3-4. All the joists are installed by attaching them to the L from below, making it easy to make changes to the layout at any stage of construction. It also easy to move, add, remove, and relocate a joist after the layout is complete without disturbing anything on top of the layout. In addition to simple alterations, L-girder requires less precise

Here's a list of tools you'll find useful for benchwork and layout construction. You probably have many of these in your toolbox already. When using any tool, be sure to always, always wear eye protection. Follow the instructions when operating power tools.

Circular saw. Not an absolute requirement, because a standard hand saw also works, but this sure speeds cutting dimensional lumber to length. It also can make long cuts in sheet material like plywood or Masonite.

Saber saw. Use to cut plywood subroadbed. You don't need the top-of-the-line model, but spring for high-quality blades and change them when they get dull.

Power screwdriver. Along with drywall screws, a power screwdriver is the layout builder's best friend. You can substitute a drill with a Phillips screwdriver bit and buy only one tool.

Power drill. The third, and final, indispensable, power tool. A variable-speed reversible model with a ⅜" chuck will handle most jobs. Use a Phillips bit to substitute for the power screwdriver, although you'll find having a drill and a screwdriver eliminates the need to change bits and speeds things along nicely.

Clamps. Buy about twice as many clamps as you think you'll need. You'll still find that you're always one short! Clamps make it easy to hold everything in place while you check alignment and level before securing everything together. I have used C-clamps for years, but for my new home layout I found Quick-Clamps to be easier to use. They are, however, a little more expensive.

Measuring tape. Get one that will allow you to measure the longest dimension in the room without interruption. I've found a 25-footer to be more than adequate for my purposes. Also, stay away from the really flimsy ones. Use the type with the lock and self-retracting tape that stays stiff and rigid. Remember the old carpenter's adage: Measure twice and cut once!

Level. You'll need one, especially if you're building a layout in a basement, where floors almost always slope. A 2-foot and a 4-foot carpenter's level are my choices.

Carpenter's square: A medium (24" per leg) square is more than adequate. Besides using it to square the legs to the benchwork, you can also use it to check the backdrop and layout corners for square.

Marking pencils. Note the plural! After spending 15 minutes looking for my one pencil (it was behind my ear!) I went to the lumber yard and got a handful of pencils and placed them all over the basement. Now there's a good chance one of them is within arm's reach when I need it.

Hammer. I don't recommend nailing benchwork together, and after you try drywall screws you won't want to! But a standard framing hammer is handy for inserting carriage bolts and T-nuts into legs.

Wrenches. Used to tighten the nuts holding the legs in place.

Motor tool. A motor tool looks like a one-handed drill and sounds like the dreaded implement used by dentists. It's ideal for cutting through soft metal, although I've also used mine to carve Styrofoam to shape and drill holes for feeder wires. Dremel is one popular brand you'll find in many hobby shops.

Utility knife. A utility knife with a fresh blade is useful for cutting thin materials such as cork, Homasote, foam core, and Masonite hardboard.

Wire strippers. This is really two tools in one: a wire cutter and a stripper for removing insulation from a piece of wire. You can strip insulation with a knife, but wire strippers make the job easier and safer.

Pliers. A medium-sized pair of needle-nose pliers is useful for bending wire around terminal posts, plus a bunch of other uses too numerous to list.

Hot glue gun. This tool forces a small amount of hot glue through a nozzle. When the glue cools it creates a stronger bond than cold glue; better still, it sets up much more quickly. I use mine for all sorts of jobs, such as attaching two pieces of wood together when I don't want a screwhead showing.

Surform rasp. This looks like a cheese grater with a handle but it works like a large file or wood rasp. I use mine to knock the heavy splinters from the edges of plywood. It's also useful for shaping foam scenery.

Safety goggles. Perhaps the single most important "tools" you own are your eyes. Take care of them. Wear eye protection when working around power tools or with any chemicals that may splash and enter your eyes. Goggles are cheap—so cheap, I keep a pair wrapped around the cord to each power tool I own. That way I can't plug the tool in without being reminded to wear eye protection.

Shop vac. You'll feel much better about your layout and you'll enjoy the hobby more if you have a clean, orderly layout room. Nothing dampens my enthusiasm more than a long clean-up session before I can get to work on the layout. The shop vac, along with a roll-around tool cart, helps keep things neat and clean. The rule is simple: Before stopping work on the layout I spend five minutes with the shop vac. Tools go in the roll-around cart which fits neatly out of the way under the benchwork. Keeping things clean will also help in the domestic relations department.

---

cutting and fitting than open-grid construction, meaning that you don't have to make precise cuts. Finally, since L-girder was designed especially to support model railroads, there is no wasted material. All the components contribute to the strength of the finished layout. Figure 3-5 shows an easy way to create the L-girders themselves.

One note on locating legs with L-girder framework: While the most natural location for legs is at the corners of a table, with L-girder you'll find it best to locate the leg assemblies about one-fifth of the way in from the ends of the girders. Also, set the legs in at least a foot from any area where the layout will be viewed and operated regularly. This will make the legs much sturdier and less likely to be kicked.

Lightweight materials

In recent years we've seen a real increase in the number of layouts constructed using lightweight materials. This is particularly apparent among portable layouts and modules. It's also becoming common among modelers who live in apartments where the mess and noise of conventional construction and materials make their use impractical.

Chief among materials used for lightweight layouts is Styrofoam insulation. This rigid insulation comes in blue, pink, gray, or green, depending on what part of the country you live in. It's most important that you use rigid insulation, since the white beaded-board Styrofoam used for small coolers and as packaging in electronics does not have the structural strength to provide a reliable base for track. Styrofoam comes in thicknesses of 1, 2, and 3 inches. It's easy to carve and shape, although it's difficult to get smooth transitions needed for grades.

Recently, Woodland Scenics released a complete Styrofoam layout "kit" that includes precut roadbed material with 2 and 3 percent grades already pre-made.

Perhaps the biggest disadvantage of Styrofoam as a benchwork material is cost. It's currently the most expensive choice. But in those cases where cost isn't a problem, as with a small layout or module, Styrofoam benchwork may be just what you're looking for.

Which benchwork method is the best?

Open-grid benchwork is ideal for small layouts, especially when the right tools are available to ensure accurate cuts. This method provides an ideal base for solid-top or cookie-cutter construction, although I feel it's a case of overkill for layouts with lots of countryside and narrow plywood subroadbed. The frame members make it easy to attach a shelf to the edge of the layout,

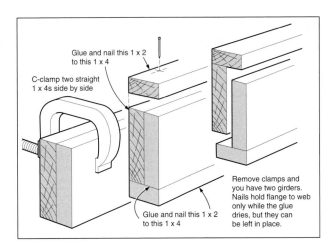

Fig. 3-5 **Making L-girders**

although that same frame makes it difficult to achieve a curved "flowing" look on the layout.

In my opinion, most model railroaders would do best with L-girder benchwork with open-frame construction and plywood subroadbed. These provide the best choices for ease of construction, strength, and versatility. Future changes to the layout, even the most major, are fairly simple to execute, and a large L-girder layout can be built in a weekend by one or two modelers armed with the appropriate tools and drywall screws.

A final thought on benchwork

In actuality, each method is equally good, and none of them is impossible to change. So simply gather up some tools and lumber and have at it.

Benchwork may seem like a chore, but it's not. No other part of model railroading produces a visible result as quickly as benchwork. But take your time and do a good job. Since benchwork is literally the foundation of the entire layout, you'll want to make that foundation as sturdy as possible.

BACKDROPS

Although they are not technically benchwork, you'll want to think about backdrops fairly early in your layout's construction. Otherwise, you may find yourself installing a backdrop in a scenicked layout, which can easily result in damaged scenery, structures, and other details.

A backdrop can be made from any smooth, non-porous surface. Over the years model railroaders have made backdrops from Masonite hardboard, cloth, styrene, Upsom board, drywall, and even postcard.

What it's made from doesn't matter as much as what a backdrop can do to improve the appearance of any layout. The kitchen cabinets once visible just behind my dining room layout hardly contributed to the sense of realism and the look of the Appalachian countryside I was trying to capture.

Then I added a backdrop made from inexpensive foam core, painted sky blue with some mountains and

clouds. Even though the layout was unfinished, the improvement the backdrop made in how things looked was astounding.

While you may already own some smaller tools suitable for model railroad use, you'll find that there are some specialized tools that will make model railroading easier. You can purchase these tools through your local hobby shop or from mail-order companies.

Screwdriver set. You'll need small screwdrivers for disassembly and maintenance of most locomotives and to install trucks and couplers on rolling stock. I like to use a set that offers several sizes of flat and Phillips-head tips.

Tweezers are useful for maneuvering parts too small to handle with your fingers. Find one that has the right amount of spring. Too little pressure makes it easy to close the jaws tightly. If tweezers require too much pressure to hold them closed, your hand can tire easily, making it difficult to work on a model. Also, get tweezers with sharp points, since they will pick up small parts more easily.

Hobby knives, of which X-acto is one popular brand, are useful for cutting parts to fit. Keep a conventional blade like the X-acto no. 11 in one and a flat-chisel blade such as the X-acto no. 17 in the other, since hobby knives have many uses, including trimming cork roadbed to fit, removing kit parts from the sprues, and cutting styrene and wood to size.

Needle or jeweler's files are useful for removing flash from plastic parts, and for cleaning up the ends of freshly cut rail when using flextrack. Files are available in a variety of shapes and lengths. The ones you'll use most often are a flat and round file in about 5" lengths.

Needle-nose pliers are useful for positioning larger parts, bending wire to shape, wrapping wire around terminals, and getting into hard-to-reach places.

Fig. 1 The proper tools will make building and repairing models much easier. This assortment of basic tools can be used for kit assembly, equipment maintenance, and light repairs.

Flush-cutting nippers (also called flush-cutting pliers) are useful for trimming parts from sprues. They can also be used for cutting small wire and can even be used to cut strip-wood and styrene to rough length.

Parts gripper, which is technically called a gem holder, is useful for handling small parts and screws. When the plunger in the top of the handle is depressed three small prongs emerge from the bottom. These jaws can pick up and hold small parts like nuts and screws during assembly.

Scale ruler. A scale ruler is an easy way to check the measurements when building models. It's useful for plastic kit assembly and absolutely required for scratchbuilding. Although most N scale models are small, get a 12"-long metal ruler that has markings for HO, S, and O scale in addition to N scale.

Artist's brushes. Besides their obvious use of painting models, artist's brushes are useful for applying liquid cement to styrene models as well as applying weathering chalks and washes.

Machinist's square. A small machinist's square will make sure those 90 degree corners are really 90 degrees. It also serves as a great jig to hold parts at right angles to each other as you're assembling models.

Other tools

While the preceding tools will get you off to a good start you'll find that after you've been in the hobby for a while you'll discover other useful tools in addition to the basic group. A few of these additional tools are shown in fig. 2.

Razor saw. A straight-bladed saw with fine teeth. A razor saw can make fine cuts very accurately and is capable of cutting any material used in model railroading. For making angled cuts you may also want to acquire a miter box. This is a handy cutting guide for the saw. Be sure to get a miter box deep enough to accept the entire saw blade.

Rail nippers are the easiest and best way to cut flexible track to length. They are so useful I'd suggest they be the first tool you purchase if you plan to use flextrack. The pair shown here is available from Micro Engineering. Resist the temptation to use your rail nippers to cut other materials. Use them only for rail and you'll be treated to a neat cut every time.

Soldering iron. You'll need a small soldering iron in the 30- to 40-watt range for wiring your layout, making

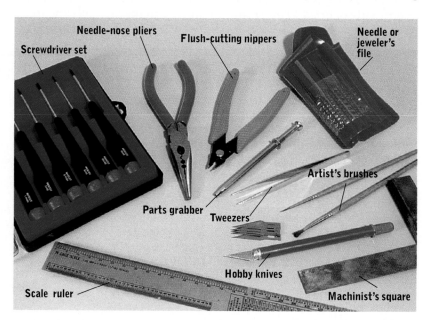

Needle-nose pliers
Screwdriver set
Flush-cutting nippers
Needle or jeweler's file
Parts grabber
Artist's brushes
Tweezers
Hobby knives
Scale ruler
Machinist's square

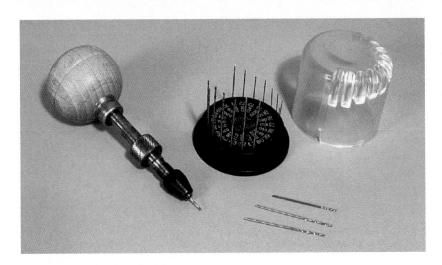

Fig. 3 **A pin vise can drill extremely small holes in soft materials like plastic, resin, and even thin sheets of brass.**

electrical repairs, and making alterations to motive power (such as installing Digital Command Control). Use only rosin-core solder for electrical work (60/40 solder is the preferred type for most electrical work). Don't use acid-core solder for electrical connections. The rosin is important since it acts as a cleaning agent, removing surface impurities, and ensuring a tight bond. Always use flux when soldering. Failure to use flux is asking for poor solder joints.

Clamps come in various sizes and shapes. Use them to hold pieces in place before applying adhesive. Then remove the clamps after the joint sets. Clamps are also handy for holding an item when soldering or for those operations when you need another hand and don't have a willing family member nearby!

Desprung nippers are available from PBL and are ideal for removing delicate plastic parts from sprues. If you plan to build any N scale rolling stock kits I recommend you acquire a set of these.

Self-closing tweezers are useful for holding parts while painting and detailing. They come in a variety of lengths, tip styles, and jaw strengths.

Scriber. Useful for marking stripwood or styrene prior to cutting the part to length.

Tap holder and taps are necessary for threading a hole to take a screw. Make sure you use the correct tap to match the size of screw you plan to use.

Body putty is a handy way to fill any unsightly gaps in the joints between pieces of a model. Apply a small quantity, let it dry completely, then sand it smooth.

Sanding sticks are flexible sticks covered with various grades of fine sandpaper. Using several grades of paper will allow you to polish a surface to a smooth, glossy finish.

Pin vise. This is one tool that deserves special mention (fig. 3). It's essentially a miniature handheld drill. Despite its name, a pin vise is used to hold small drill bits. You turn it by hand to drill holes in plastic, wood, or even thin metal. A pin vise can also be used to hold a tap for threading holes. Along with the pin vise you'll need a set of drill bits. An assortment of bits ranging from no. 6 to no. 80 is ideal

Adhesives. The type of adhesive depends upon the material you'll be joining. The three most common glues are liquid cement, used for styrene; white or yellow glue, which can be used for wood and paper models; and cyanoacrylate adhesive (CA), more commonly known as "super glue," for joining almost everything else.

Motor tool. If you have only one power tool for modeling, this should be the one. You can use a motor tool to cut, polish, sand, grind, and shape. Always wear safety goggles when operating a motor tool.

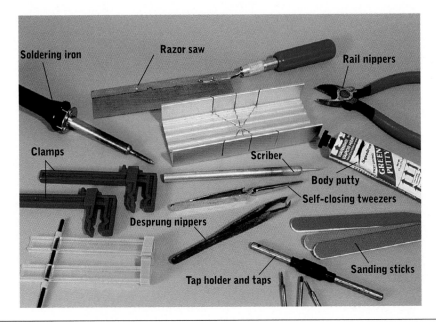

Fig. 2 **You may want to add these tools to your basic tool kit, especially if you plan to do much scratchbuilding or kitbashing. The rail nippers are almost essential for laying flextrack.**

Soldering iron

Razor saw

Rail nippers

Clamps

Scriber

Body putty

Self-closing tweezers

Desprung nippers

Sanding sticks

Tap holder and taps

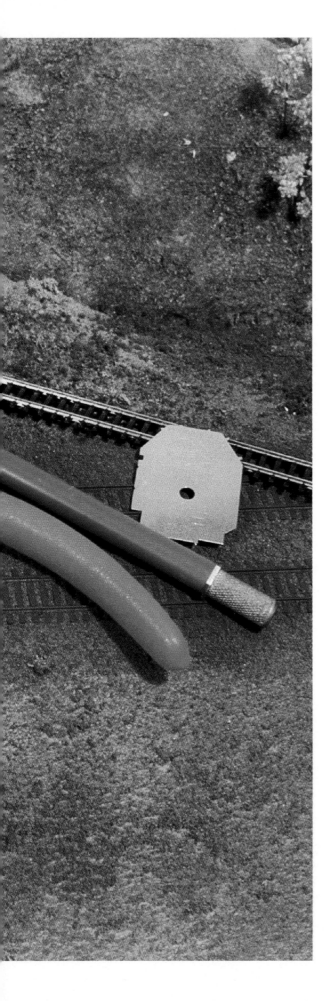

CHAPTER FOUR

TRACK

From Roadbed to Golden Spike

Tracklaying is perhaps the most critical single phase of layout construction. Without good, reliable trackwork, even the best-looking model railroad will prove to be a disappointment. But since many of us are anxious to get things rolling, we often use less care when laying track than we should. The result is a layout that doesn't run well, if it runs at all. That's why I encourage you to take your time when laying the track. It's easier, cheaper, and in the long run faster to take your time and do it right the first time. Otherwise you'll end up ripping up completed scenery and track to fix a problem.

It's also important to keep in mind that track is a model. Like anything else we want to model it's important to know something about the prototype before attempting to build a model. Figure 4-1 shows some typical prototype track.

An amazing variety of track products are available in N scale, making it possible to duplicate almost any prototype track arrangement. With a little care and some weathering and ballast, N scale track can look as good as that in larger scales. And since a large N scale layout allows room for truly broad curves and gentle switches, some modelers handlay switches and track to achieve startlingly realistic results.

Model railroad track must work flawlessly and look realistic. This chapter will get you started on achieving both of these goals.

Easements and curves

Before actually laying any track, you'll want to consider your minimum radius. As a general rule, always use the broadest curves possible. You'll also want to plan for easements for all the curves. If your curves are very sharp, say 9", long-wheel-base equipment such as six-axle diesel locomotives, larger steam engines, and passenger cars will have trouble negotiating the curve. They'll either bind or derail. Even if they manage to get through those tight curves, the added drag on the locomotive may result in jerky operation. In addition to the operational requirements you also need to consider appearance (fig. 4-2).

Large-radius curves simply look better, and in turn the entire layout looks better. As we discussed in the chapter on planning a layout, always use the broadest curves possible. I'd recommend an absolute minimum of 11" radius for hidden track and no less than 15" radius curves for visible mainline track.

Along with minimum radius you need to consider easements, which I've also heard called transition spirals. This is nothing more than a short stretch of curved track with a much broader radius than the circular curve. You can get pretty fancy figuring out curve easements, and the NMRA has tables listing various easements that they recommend based on the curve radius.

You can figure out the math if you want to, but one of the best ways to get a nice smooth transition in your curves is to use a piece of molding trim that's flexible enough to bend to your minimum radius. As shown in fig. 4-3, use a radius gauge, which is simply a piece of wood with holes drilled every inch for various curve radii, and draw a circular curve.

Once the curve is in place, draw a center line for the tangent, or straight track, but don't connect it directly to the line for the curve (fig. 4-4). Offset it slightly (about ⅛" to ¼" for most typical N scale curves). Then take flexible molding and tack it in place along the curve. Bend it until it lines up with the tangent line and trace a line along the molding connecting the curved and tangent lines (fig. 4-5). The natural bend of the wood creates a workable transition spiral.

Roadbed

Now that you've drawn the center lines for your track, there's one more consideration before track-laying. We need to discuss roadbed. You could lay the track directly to your subroadbed material, but there are a number of reasons you'll want to consider using roadbed.

Roadbed helps reduce the noise of trains running on track attached directly to the plywood or Styrofoam subroadbed. In addition, it contributes to realism. Prototype track, especially mainline track, is raised above the surrounding terrain to assist in drainage. Several commercial roadbed products are available at the hobby shop, or you can cut your own roadbed from larger sheet material. The simplest to use are cork roadbed, Vinylbed, and AMSI Instant-Roadbed. Cork and Vinylbed are installed much the same way. The cork comes already precut. Peel the two halves apart and then lay the inside seam of the one section of cork against the track center line. Then lay the second half of the cork in place. It's a good

---

LAYING AMSI INSTANT ROADBED

Instant roadbed is easy to use and forms an ideal roadbed for N scale layouts. One of chief advantages of this product is that you can lay track simply by pressing it into place on the roadbed material, eliminating the need for nails, spikes, or glue. This arrangement is fairly permanent, but you can remove the track from the roadbed with some careful prying after you press it in place. Before the track or roadbed is firmly adhered it's fairly easy to move the Instant Roadbed around if you have to make some slight adjustments.

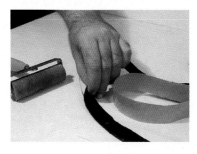

Step 1. AMSI Instant Roadbed is a butylated rubber product that's sticky on both sides. Apply it first to the sub-roadbed following the track center line you drew previously.

Step 2. Use a roller and a fair amount of pressure to make the roadbed adhere to the subroadbed material (in this case ½" plywood). Placing the waxed paper over the roadbed material will prevent the roller from sticking to the roadbed.

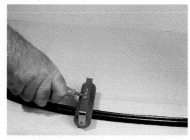

Step 3. Position the track on the Instant Roadbed and get it aligned properly. The track will stick to the roadbed but minor adjustment is still possible. Once you're satisfied with the track's placement, use a roller to press it into place.

idea to overlap the seams slightly on the ends, especially on curves. This prevents the cork from developing a kink.

To install the cork roadbed for turnouts you can purchase ready-made cork turnout sections or make your own by laying the cork through the straight leg of the turnout. Then line up the second section through the angled portion of the turnout, allowing the cork to overlap the straight section. Use a sharp hobby knife to trim the cork to shape.

Vinylbed is installed in much the same way as cork, except that the roadbed comes in one-piece sections. You'll have to take a little more care to install the roadbed along the track center line.

Either the cork or vinyl roadbed can be secured to the plywood or Styrofoam using nails or adhesive. Although many modelers use Liquid Nails or contact cement, I use yellow carpenter's glue. I spread a small amount of glue along the track center line, lay the roadbed in place, and trim it to fit. If the subroadbed is plywood, I use small brads to hold the roadbed in place until the glue sets. For Styrofoam layouts I use map pins to hold the roadbed in position until the glue sets. Then I remove the map pins. The result is a solid base ready for track.

Another roadbed material you'll want to be familiar with is AMSI Instant Roadbed. It's a rubber product that never dries out. It's sticky on both sides. Installation of AMSI roadbed is described on page 26.

Tracklaying

There are several ways to lay N scale track. You can handlay your track in the same manner as

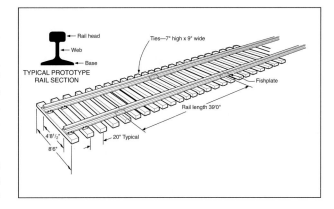

4-1. Prototype track dimensions and nomenclature

4-2. Long cars and locomotives look unrealistic on sharp curves. Also, they often don't perform well around such tight corners.

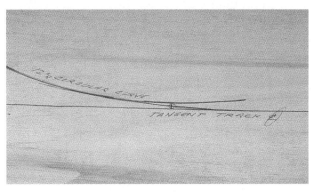

4-3. You can make a good compass for tracklaying from a piece of scrap 1 x 2 with a nail in one end. Drill holes for each radius you plan to use. Then tack the nail in place on the layout and draw the curve with a pencil. Christine Paul

4-4. You can create a workable easement by offsetting the center lines of the circular curve and the tangent (straight) track by a small amount. Then draw a freehand line at a gradual radius connecting the two.

4-5. A flexible piece of molding makes it easy to create transition spirals directly on the layout. Lay the molding on the curve and offset the tangent slightly. The natural curve of the molding provides a useful spiral easement. Christine Paul

4-6. Sectional track is the first type of track most modelers encounter. The Bachmann E-Z Track (bottom) comes with plastic roadbed, which eliminates the need to ballast the completed track. Standard Atlas sectional track is at the top.

4-7. Several manufacturers offer flexible track. The three most popular brands are, top to bottom, Atlas, Peco, and Micro Engineering.

prototype railroads, with individual wood ties and rail. Since spikes would interfere with the wheel flanges on most N scale rolling stock, most hand-laid N scale track is secured to the ties using adhesive. Many modelers who chose to handlay track use ties cut from printed circuit board. The rail is then soldered to these ties. One of the chief advantages of handlaid track is the ability to custom-build turnouts to fit the situation. If you don't want to build your own turnouts completely from scratch, pre-made frogs and kits for complete turnouts are available. The techniques needed to handlay track are often explained in detailed articles in *Model Railroader*. I'd advise staying away from handlaid track on your first N scale layout, since you may have a tendency to rush more than you should. But consider it for a future layout.

The easiest way to lay track on an N scale layout is to use sectional track (fig. 4-6). This is the type of track included with many train sets, and since sectional track is the easiest to work with, it's often the best choice for your first layout.

Manufacturers of sectional track have made a number of improvements over the years. Newer types of sectional track come mounted to plastic roadbed components that get the track (and more important, the locomotive gears) up and away from the carpet. These sections also ensure positive mechanical and electrical contact.

Since the curves that come with sectional track are pretty limiting, and since sectional track looks toylike, the most popular choice for N scale is flexible track (fig. 4-7).

Flextrack is a special type of sectional track sold in sections approximately 3 feet long (the exact length varies among manufacturers.) These sections can be laid straight or bent to almost any curve. There are spaces in the molded tie strip under the rails that allow the track to flex. Flextrack allows you to achieve a more realistic appearance for your layout since you aren't limited to fixed-radius curves as you are with sectional track.

Flextrack made by different manufacturers has different characteristics, so you may want to experiment a little to see which one you find easiest to work with. Atlas and Peco track sections are much more flexible than those sold by Micro Engineering. The chief difference is the way the track acts when it's bent. Micro Engineering track will take the curve and hold it without being fastened in place. Atlas and Peco track will flex back to their natural position unless the track is secured. Many N scale modelers I've met prefer to use Micro Engineering track for visible areas and Atlas or Peco for hidden track and staging yards.

One disadvantage of using flextrack, especially for beginners, is the need to cut the rail to length. When you curve a section of flextrack the rail ends will be uneven, meaning that the longer one must be cut flush with the shorter one. Also, you frequently need to cut the 3-foot sections into shorter pieces to create particular track arrangements.

You'll often hear the term "code" associated with rail. This is simply a way of indicating the height of the rail in thousandths of an inch. For example, code 55 rail is .055" high. Code 80 rail is .080" tall. Code 55 rail is the size closest to the typical North American prototype that has turnouts readily available. Code 40 flextrack is the closest to true scale size for N scale, but there are no code 40 turnouts. If you want to use smaller rail you should be aware that cars and locomotives with deep flanges will not operate properly on code 40 or even code 55 rail. Most N scale diesels and some steam locomotives can run on code 55, but for code 40 operation the flanges may have to be turned down, an advanced operation not recommended for beginners. You'll be safe with code 55, provided you don't plan to operate older N scale locomotives and are prepared to replace the wheelsets on some of the more inexpensive freight and passenger cars with wheels that have narrower flanges.

Some people find code 55 rail a little too flimsy to work with or find that it doesn't hold up well to cleaning. If that's the case, but you still want the

4-8. Flexible track must be cut to fit properly. Use a pair of rail nippers to cut the track to length.

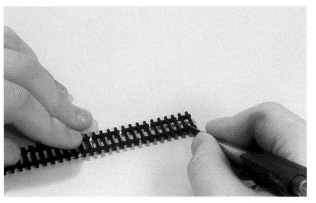

4-9. Square the rail ends using a small file. Christine Paul

appearance of code 55 rail, I'd suggest using Peco code 55 flextrack and turnouts. By using a double web on the base of the rail, Peco code 70 rail is buried in the ties, leaving .055" exposed above the ties. This arrangement creates code 55 visible rail with the same strength as code 70. When the track is ballasted and weathered you can't see the deeper rail. It's an ideal compromise for modelers who want good-looking track that's also rugged. Best of all, Peco also offers a complete line of code 55 turnouts that are made the same way as the flextrack.

It's possible, with some care, to connect Micro Engineering flextrack to Peco turnouts. This opens up the best of both worlds. The sidebar on page 30 shows how to do this.

Tracklaying tips

Now that the preliminary work is out of the way, it's time to lay some iron. Here are a few tips that will serve you well when you're laying the track on your layout:
• The track must be in proper gauge at all times.
• Rail ends should be matched perfectly, with no gaps, misalignments, or kinks.
• Straight track should blend into curves with some sort of transition curve or easement. This is simply a short length of track at each end of the

CLEANING TRACK

Dirty track is one of the leading causes of poor operation in any scale. With the small size and light weight of N scale trains, dirty track can be a particularly big problem. The best solution is prevention. Having a ceiling in the layout room and keeping the room free of construction debris and other dust will help prevent track from getting dirty in the first place. But a little track cleaning will be necessary.

After construction, especially after ballasting and other scenery work, it will be necessary to really clean the surface of the rails. For this heavy cleaning I recommend a hard track cleaner, such as a Bright Boy, that

you run along the top and inside surfaces of the rails.

Track-cleaning cars are an easy way to keep the rails polished with little effort. Aztec track-cleaning cars (left) consist of a Micro-Trains car body that's been specially modified with a hard roller to clean the track as it runs. The Centerline (right) cars have a solid brass frame with Micro-Trains (or Rapido) trucks and couplers. A metal roller, wrapped in a cloth, rolls along the track when it's pushed (or pulled) by a locomotive. You can soak the cloth in liquid track cleaner or run the car with a dry pad.

Both these cars offer an easy way to keep the rails polished, letting you run some trains in the process.

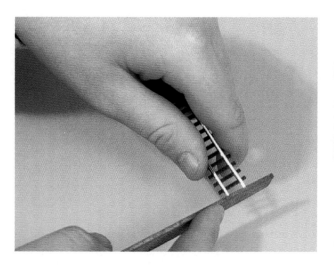

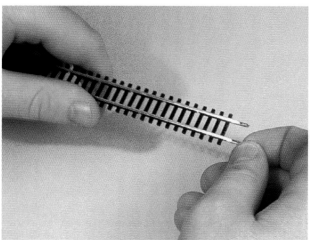

4-10. Use a hobby knife to trim away the ties on the end of the rail.

4-11. Slip the rail joiner over the base of the rail.

constant-radius curve that has an infinite radius. It allows for smooth flow of trains into curves without a sudden lurching that can cause operating problems.

Before laying the track, you need to consider how you'll be securing the track to the roadbed. There are three basic methods (1) gluing it down, (2) nailing it in place, and (3) using the adhesive on the Instant Roadbed. Since the most common of these three techniques is driving small wire nails (½" no. 18 are a good choice) through holes in the center of the plastic tie strip, that's the method I'll explain here. For tips on gluing track

in place, see the tracklaying section of the Carolina Central project layout.

Most N scale track comes with holes predrilled in the center of the ties. If yours doesn't, you can drill your own using a pin vise with a no. 60 drill bit. A faster method is to use a motor tool to create nail holes. If you decide to use a motor tool, be careful to not melt the ties.

Laying flextrack takes some practice, but it's not difficult. Figures 4-8 through 4-11 show how to prepare a piece of flextrack.

Although straight track is pretty straightforward, curves can be a little trickier. When laying a

JOINING PECO AND MICRO ENGINEERING TRACK

As most N scalers can tell you, Micro-Engineering track looks nice but Peco track offers a much greater variety of turnouts, including curves, wyes, and slip switches. Currently Micro-Engineering only offers no. 6 turnouts.

Peco streamlined code 55 track is not really code 55 rail. Instead, it cleverly uses code 70 rail with an extra flange. The result is the rigidity of code 70 rail with the appearance of code 55.

But that presents a problem when joining the Peco track to "conventional" rail like that used by Micro Engineering.

The usual trick of flattening one end of a rail joiner and soldering the adjoining rail didn't seem the right answer since Peco's ties are thicker (about .030") than Micro-Engineering's.

The solution sounds complex but is really very simple. First, trim the ties back from the end of the Peco track. Then, using a cutoff disk in a Dremel tool (Please, please wear eye protection for this!) cut into the Peco rail far enough to slip a Micro-Engineering code 55 rail joiner, flush with the bottom web of the code 55 rail (see diagram). Then cut away the lower web and file the track to true code 55. Then use three shims of .010" styrene to even up the ties and join the Peco and Micro-Engineering track together with a M/E code 55 rail joiner.

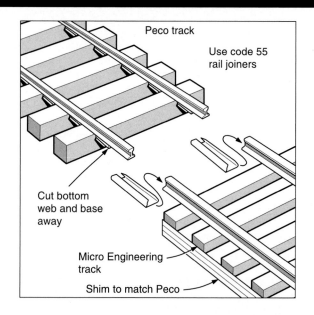

Peco track

Use code 55 rail joiners

Cut bottom web and base away

Micro Engineering track

Shim to match Peco

The result was an easy way to combine the varied geometry of Peco turnouts with the appearance of Micro-Engineering. And while the ties are different dimensions, once the rail is painted and ballasted the difference is hard to spot. In fact, you'll have to show visitors where the joints between the two brands or track are.

curve with flextrack, tack down one end with a brad, then lay the track into the curve. If the section of flextrack makes it all the way through the curve, cut the two rails even with each other and tack the rest of the section in place. More often, you'll find you need a rail joint in the arc of the curve itself. Lay the section of flextrack through the first part of the curve as normal, but leave the last 5" to 7" of track straight. Trim the rail ends flush and add the next section of flextrack. Solder the rail joint, allow the solder to cool, and file the joint smooth before continuing the track through the remainder of the curve.

When nailing the track in place, never tap or press the nails down to tie top level. Driving the nail completely home in this manner can bend the tie down, pulling the rail out of gauge.

Sight along the rail frequently to make sure there are no kinks between sections of rail. Joints between track sections should be seamless. If you can see a kink, you can be sure you'll have operational problems in those areas.

When laying flextrack, make sure the curves are smooth and of a constant radius through the entire curve. Make certain that switch points move freely after installation. Use only a few brads to hold the switches in place. This lets the switch "float," reducing the chance of binding. You'll also want to be sure that the points are resting tightly against the stock rails, and that the two are at the same height. You may have to use a small file to adjust this fit slightly.

Turnouts

Turnouts, commonly called "switches," are used to route a train from one track to another. Figure 4-12 shows the individual parts of an N scale turnout. Turnouts are one of the biggest potential source of track troubles. Trains can easily derail if a turnout isn't thrown completely, if the track is out of gauge at any point in the turnout, or if the frog is fouled.

Although we use the word "turnout," real railroads call these tracks "switches." Since model railroaders also use electrical switches to control track power, if you tell someone to throw the "switch for the yard lead" it may be unclear if you're referring to the electrical switch or the points on the turnout. "Throw the turnout for the yard lead" makes it clear you're talking about track.

Turnouts are identified by the direction of the divergent (curved) route, either right or left, as well as by frog number. A turnout frog number confuses a lot of people, but it's really quite simple. It's a measure of units. If a turnout diverges one unit for six units of run, we call this a "Number 6" turnout. If it diverges one unit in four units of run, we call it a Number 4. A turnout that diverges equally in both directions, so that it's shaped like the letter "Y" is called a "wye."

The three most common brands of ready-made commercial turnouts are Atlas, Peco, and Micro-

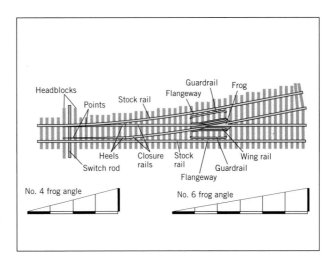

4-12. The key components of an N scale turnout

4-13. A final light misting of Polly Scale Earth and Grimy Black blends the ballast and track together. A heavy concentration of black on the turnout points and in areas where locomotives sit (and leak oil) is a realistic touch.

Engineering. Bachmann also offers a right and left turnout with its "Easy Track" system.

Most N scale turnouts work well right out of the box, but it never hurts to do a little fine-tuning before installing them on the layout. Since many turnouts have a slight upward bulge about halfway along the length, use a fine-cut mill file to carefully smooth this out. I also use a small file to gently file the ends of the point so they blend into the stock rails. This helps prevent the wheels from "picking" the points, the most common cause of derailments when going through turnouts. Also check the height of the point rail where it meets the stock rail. If the point is higher, file the point rail flush. Finally, check and make sure the frog is free of burrs and obstructions. On plastic frogs, I use a sharp knife for this. With metal frogs, like those on Micro-Engineering turnouts, I use a small file.

Once you're convinced the turnout is working smoothly, you're ready to install it on the layout.

CHAPTER FIVE

WIRING AND TRAIN CONTROL

Many beginning model railroaders believe you need some sort of special knowledge of electricity to wire a layout. In fact, you can wire a layout without knowing the first thing about electrical theory, simply by following step-by-step instructions or through trial and error. I'm going to offer some practical suggestions on wiring a layout in the hopes it will inspire you to tackle this phase of layout construction without fear. But there's no way I can hope to cover such a complex topic as layout wiring in a single short chapter. If you're interested in learning more about model railroad wiring I highly recommend reading *Easy Model Railroad Wiring* by *Model Railroader* editor Andy Sperandeo. Andy offers a small smattering of electrical theory and chapter after chapter of knowledge gained through first-hand experience wiring model railroads.

Mark Watson built the N scale Arkansas & Missouri as a project layout for *Model Railroader.* He used conventional cab control wiring with walkaround throttles to control the trains. Mark made that attractive control panel using his computer.

Fig. 5-1 You'll want to replace your train set power pack with a better model, like this one from MRC. A great number of features are available.

Train control

Train control units, commonly called power packs, throttles, or transformers, come in an assortment of shapes and sizes in a wide price range. If you started with a train set, it probably came with a small power pack with very little power output and poor speed control. Power packs vary widely in quality and price. Smaller, underpowered packs may have moving parts that don't stand up and electrical parts too skimpy for the load, meaning that they can't control double-headed trains or provide enough current to a train of lighted passenger cars.

Choose a power pack that can power all the locomotives needed to pull the longest train you plan to run (fig. 5-1). The exact rating of the pack will vary depending upon the size of the layout and the planned operation. As a general rule, you want the power pack to deliver .2 ampere for each locomotive to be operated simultaneously plus .05 ampere for each grain-of-wheat lamp. That .2 ampere is only an average. To determine the exact current draw you must measure the current drawn by each locomotive when it's running at 12 volts.

A common rating for an N scale power pack is 1 ampere at 12 volts (12 watts), which is adequate for most home layouts. Larger layouts, such as club layouts and modular setups, will require power packs with higher power ratings.

Some of the better power packs include exotic features such as momentum control, separate braking features, "pulse" control, and changing the response of motors when both starting and changing loads.

Safety

While the low-voltage electricity used to control N scale trains is not dangerous, the 115-volt AC house wiring that power packs operate with is dangerous and can be deadly. This 115-volt AC power is present in the terminals of the transformer inside the power pack casing. For that reason opening the power pack case and attempting repairs or modifications is not only a violation of the warranty, it's also dangerous. Periodically inspect the cord for worn or frayed wires and make sure you turn off or unplug the power pack when it's not in use.

Wiring for one-train conventional DC operation

One-train wiring is quite simple and basic. Run two wires from the variable DC output terminal on the back of the power pack to the track as shown in fig. 5-2. You can obtain suitable wire from most hobby shops or electronics supply stores such as Radio Shack.

There are several ways to get electricity from the wires into the rails. The most reliable method is by soldering the wires directly to the rails. Always use 60/40 rosin core solder for any electrical work on your layout.

Most sectional track manufacturers offer terminal track sections, which have screws mounted to the ties. Simply attach the wires to the screws, and you're done. I don't like the terminal sections since they look out of place on a scenicked layout. Instead, I use terminal rail joiners (fig. 5-3).

These are simply standard rail joiners with short lengths of feeder wire already soldered in place. Drill a hole in the layout, slip the rail joiner onto the track, and run the wire through the hole,

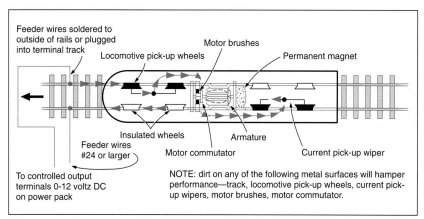

Feeder wires soldered to outside of rails or plugged into terminal track

Motor brushes

Locomotive pick-up wheels

Permanent magnet

Insulated wheels

Armature

Feeder wires #24 or larger

Motor commutator

Current pick-up wiper

To controlled output terminals 0-12 voltz DC on power pack

NOTE: dirt on any of the following metal surfaces will hamper performance—track, locomotive pick-up wheels, current pick-up wipers, motor brushes, motor commutator.

Fig. 5-2 Components of a basic train control circuit

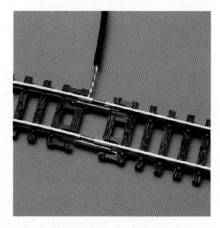

Fig. 5-3 Using terminal rail joiners

connecting it with the wires from the power pack.

On small oval layouts you only need to connect one pair of wires to the track anywhere on the oval. For larger oval layouts it's a good idea to add a feeder wire (5-4) at the opposite side of the layout. Without feeders, the train's speed will drop when it's far away from the wires and speed up as it gets closer.

Wiring a layout with turnouts requires special consideration. For example, Atlas and some Peco N scale turnouts are wired so both routes through the turnout are powered, regardless of the position of the points. Other brands such as Micro Engineering turnouts are power-routing, meaning that the switch points route electrical power as well as the train. Layouts with power-routing turnouts must be wired with feeders at the point end of the turnouts as shown in fig. 5-5.

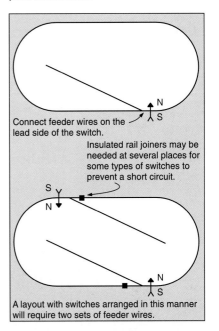

Fig. 5-4 **(Left) Feeder wire locations on simple plans**

Fig. 5-5 **(Below) Feeder wire locations on plans with switches**

Connect feeder wires on the lead side of the switch.

Insulated rail joiners may be needed at several places for some types of switches to prevent a short circuit.

A layout with switches arranged in this manner will require two sets of feeder wires.

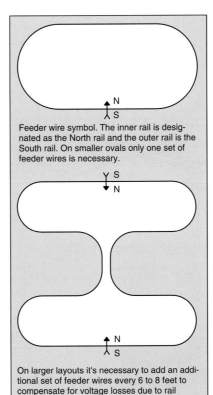

Feeder wire symbol. The inner rail is designated as the North rail and the outer rail is the South rail. On smaller ovals only one set of feeder wires is necessary.

On larger layouts it's necessary to add an additional set of feeder wires every 6 to 8 feet to compensate for voltage losses due to rail resistence.

Wiring for two-train operation

If running one train is fun, then it stands to reason that running two trains at once must be twice as much fun. How can you accomplish this without resorting to advanced forms of layout control? There are several methods, but the best choice is through the use of "dual-cab control." To wire a layout for dual cab control you must first divide the track into electrically isolated sections called "blocks." Figure 5-6 shows how dual-cab control works.

Note that track in each of the two blocks shown is wired to the center terminals of a single-pole, double-throw (DPDT) center-off toggle switch. The upper terminals on the toggle switches are connected to the power pack on the left, which we'll call Cab A, while the lower terminals on the switch are connected to the pack on the right (Cab B). When the toggle switch is up, Cab A controls the block. When the toggle is in the down position Cab B has control of the block. Setting the switch in the center turns off all power to the block, which is useful for places like locomotive terminals where you'll want to park locomotives without someone accidentally turning one on from across the room.

To wire a layout for dual cab control you need to isolate the sections of track from one another. You can do this with specially made plastic insulated rail joiners. These work well, except that you need to know where all the gaps will be as you're laying the track. Another method is to cut gaps with a cutoff disk in a motor tool (fig. 5-7). Be sure to wear eye protection when cutting the rail. As the drawing shows, you can fill the gap

with a small piece of styrene secured with cyanoacrylate adhesive (CA). The plastic can be filed to shape after the cement dries and then painted to match the rail.

You may have noticed in fig. 5-6 that only one of the two rails has a gap. We can reduce the amount of work required to wire a layout by taking advantage of the fact that current needs to flow along one rail, into the locomotive through the wheels, and back out the other side before leaving the locomotive through the opposite rail and returning to the power pack. To control power to any block all we need do is gap one of the two rails—thereby controlling the current flow to the locomotive. The other rail is left ungapped. This method of wiring is called "common rail." One rule about common rail wiring—be consistent. You can choose either rail to be "common," but make sure you don't get mixed up as you're wiring the layout and get the common and gapped rails confused.

Dual-cab operation is fine for smaller layouts. It's also fine for larger layouts. One piece of advice: Try to keep the blocks as large as possible without detracting from your planned operating scheme. With several trains moving it's easy to get so engrossed in throwing toggle switches that you never really watch the trains move! Operating a layout with dual-cab control is pretty straightforward. Simply repeat the wiring diagram as shown, adding a toggle switch for each block. Mount the toggle switches on the layout for easy access.

Walkaround control

Many of today's larger layouts are designed with long main lines that run along aisles to create

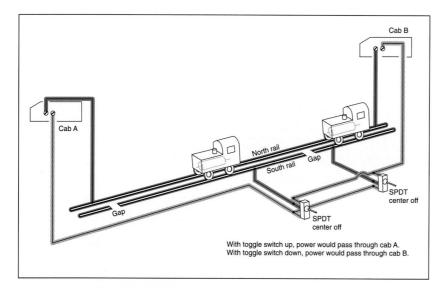

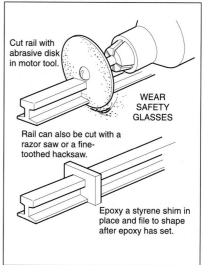

Fig. 5-6 **Cab control wiring diagram**

With toggle switch up, power would pass through cab A.
With toggle switch down, power would pass through cab B.

Fig. 5-7 **Cutting rail gaps**

Fig. 5-8 **Bill and Wayne Reid have installed easy-to-understand control panels at each town on their Cumberland Valley layout. Each throttle is color-coded so engineers know which jack to plug into.**

the impression in the viewer's mind that he is looking at the real world. Each train passes through a scene only once before moving on to the next scene. To create this illusion double-sided backdrops and multilevel layouts are becoming more and more common.

The wonderful reality created by modern layouts creates a real problem when it comes to train control. After all, what good is a centralized control panel with toggle switches and power packs when operators can't see the entire railroad? How can they control their trains?

The solution is quite simple and it has the added advantage of putting the operator as close to the action as he or she can get without climbing in the locomotive cab. Most of the layouts you see nowadays have done away with centralized control panels and permanently mounted power packs in favor of walkaround throttles.

Layout controls for switch machines and block power are mounted directly to the layout fascia. Controls for speed, direction, and braking are mounted in a small hand-held box with a cord that can be plugged into a throttle bus at one of several points on the layout. Typically, throttle jacks are located at each town. For multiple cab control color-coded jacks and throttles can be used, so by plugging the orange throttle into the orange jack you can control your train.

Now layout builders don't need to add switch motors to control every turnout or advanced detection systems. After all, the operators can throw the turnouts manually, since they're right there. And they don't need advanced detection circuitry, since they're able to see where their train is most of the time.

But even if a walkaround cab-control system is ideal for many modelers, it still requires a tremendous amount of wiring, lots of toggle switches, and a large chunk of time, most of it under the layout, connecting all those wires together.

Command control

What is command control? Rather than trying to explain how it works, perhaps it's easier to explain what it can do for you.

Since the start of the hobby we've been trying to find ways to simulate the looks and workings of prototype trains. Command control allows us to do that. It's a means of independently controlling multiple trains on the same track without the need to switch block toggles on and off.

There are basically two types of command control systems: analog and digital. Analog systems

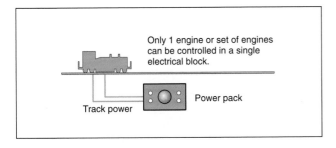

Fig. 5-9 **Conventional train control**

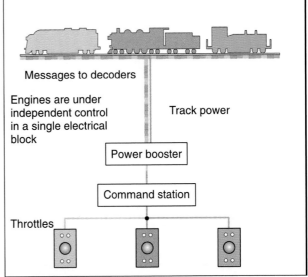

Fig. 5-10 **Typical DCC control**

are really marketed for the larger scales, HO and up, so I won't address them here. But thanks to the National Model Railroad Association's Digital Command Control (DCC) standards, command control is here to stay. And advances in electronics have made it possible to equip even the smallest N scale locomotives for command control.

Command control is basically a way of controlling electrical devices by means of a signal sent through the rails. The electrical devices that DCC controls are most often the motors inside a locomotive. With command control a constant voltage is kept on the rails. Why, therefore, doesn't that constant voltage cause every locomotive to take off out of control? To understand how this works see fig. 5-9.

With conventional DC control we aren't really controlling the trains at all. We're controlling the voltage applied to the rails, which powers the motor. We can run only one engine, or a group of engines, in a single block at one time. All those locomotives run at the same relative speed depending on how much current we apply to the rails. That's completely unlike the prototype. Real locomotive engineers can run right up to each other, and if they're not careful right into each other. The locomotive is controlled by the engineer, not by some outside power source.

Moving the means of controlling each locomotive into each individual engine is the magic of command control (fig. 5-10).

Several companies make complete DCC systems, and some companies specialize in add-on or accessory equipment. MRC, the same company that makes the power packs I mentioned earlier, offers an inexpensive entry-level DCC system called the MRC Command 2000. This system has some limitations, but it's a great way to get your feet wet without spending a lot of money. Two other companies that specialize in DCC are Digitrax and Wangrow Electronics. Digitrax offers several starter sets geared towards a range of budgets and needs such as the Empire Builder (fig. 5-11). Many hobby shops stock DCC equipment, another good sign for this part of the hobby, and several mail-order dealers specialize in selling DCC equipment.

Wiring tips

No matter whether you decide to use one-cab control or go all out with Digital Command Con-

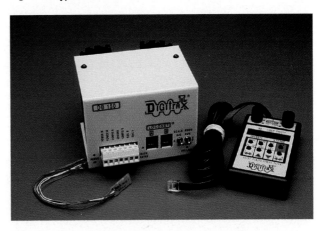

Fig. 5-11 **This is a Digitrax Empire Builder starter set. Digitrax combines the command station and the booster in one unit.**

trol, there are a few things you should keep in mind about wiring in general.

Wiring is much more than simply routing wires under the table to the control system. The way the wires are routed is at least as important as the connections themselves. First of all, neatness counts. Label each wire at every connection point. At terminal strips you can apply labels above or below the screw terminal on the layout itself. Assign a letter to each terminal strip and a number to each post and record what each wire does.

Color-coding also helps. Settle on two colors of wire for track wiring (black and red, for instance), with other colors for switch machine wiring or lamps. Don't run every wire in a dead straight line from one place to another. Instead take a circuitous route and allow more wire length than you think you'll need. You'll be glad you did if you ever need to splice into that wire in the future.

Good electrical connections are critical. Never rely on solder alone to hold a wire to a terminal. Crimp the lead around the terminal to be certain of a positive connection.

CHAPTER SIX

LOCOMOTIVES

Motive power for your railroad

When most people think of railroads, the image of a locomotive is usually the first thing that comes to mind. Locomotives have fascinated people since the first tea-kettles on rails puffed their way along at then-amazing speeds in excess of 15 miles per hour! Today, massive diesel locomotives generating thousands of horsepower race across the continent. Many modelers choose an era, or time period, for their layout based solely on the type of locomotives that operated during those years.

In this chapter we'll take a brief look at the variety of N scale locomotives available, and we'll also discuss some tips for selecting a locomotive that's right for your railroad. Then we'll discuss some basic locomotive maintenance and show how to install magnetic couplers on some of the most popular models available.

Any locomotive can be painted and relettered, making it possible to model even the less popular prototype railroads. The author detailed and painted these Atlas U-25Bs for the Maine Central.

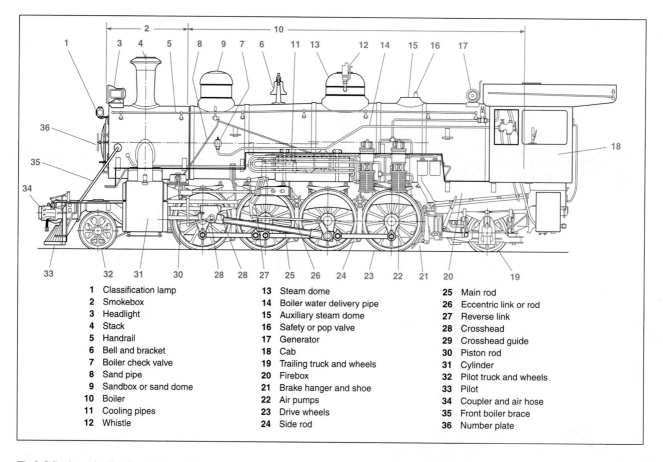

1 Classification lamp	**13** Steam dome	**25** Main rod
2 Smokebox	**14** Boiler water delivery pipe	**26** Eccentric link or rod
3 Headlight	**15** Auxiliary steam dome	**27** Reverse link
4 Stack	**16** Safety or pop valve	**28** Crosshead
5 Handrail	**17** Generator	**29** Crosshead guide
6 Bell and bracket	**18** Cab	**30** Piston rod
7 Boiler check valve	**19** Trailing truck and wheels	**31** Cylinder
8 Sand pipe	**20** Firebox	**32** Pilot truck and wheels
9 Sandbox or sand dome	**21** Brake hanger and shoe	**33** Pilot
10 Boiler	**22** Air pumps	**34** Coupler and air hose
11 Cooling pipes	**23** Drive wheels	**35** Front boiler brace
12 Whistle	**24** Side rod	**36** Number plate

Fig 6-1 Basic parts of a steam locomotive

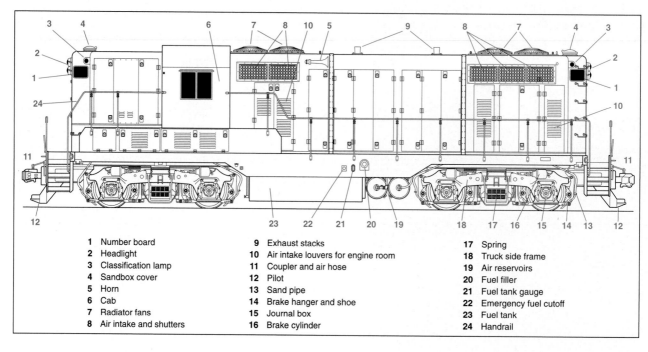

1 Number board	**9** Exhaust stacks	**17** Spring
2 Headlight	**10** Air intake louvers for engine room	**18** Truck side frame
3 Classification lamp	**11** Coupler and air hose	**19** Air reservoirs
4 Sandbox cover	**12** Pilot	**20** Fuel filler
5 Horn	**13** Sand pipe	**21** Fuel tank gauge
6 Cab	**14** Brake hanger and shoe	**22** Emergency fuel cutoff
7 Radiator fans	**15** Journal box	**23** Fuel tank
8 Air intake and shutters	**16** Brake cylinder	**24** Handrail

Fig 6-3 Basic parts of a diesel locomotive

Steam Locomotives

Steam propulsion dominated the railroad industry from its founding right up to the eve of World War II. With the nostalgic appeal and extensive selection of visible piping, valve gear, and side rods, most of which move very visibly, it's no wonder steam locomotives have always been a popular subject with model railroaders. Prototype steam locomotives are complex machines with miles of piping. Figure 6-1 shows the external parts of a typical steam locomotive.

Steam locomotives are classified by wheel arrangement using the Whyte system. The wheel arrangement tells a great deal about the use of the locomotive. In addition, many types of steam locomotives were given nicknames, which are mostly a reflection of the railroad that first ran a locomotive of a particular type. The wheel arrangement and nickname are interchangeable, but note that some wheel arrangements have two nicknames, again depending on the originating railroads.

The first number in the classification denotes the number of leading, or pony, wheels on one side of the locomotive. The second number is the number of drive wheels, which are easily identified as the wheels connected to the rod on the side of the locomotive. The third number is the number of trailing wheels. Note that a locomotive need not have all three types of wheels. When it doesn't, the number "0" is substituted in the wheel arrangement. For example, a 2-8-0 has two lead wheels, eight drive wheels (four on each side) and no trailing wheels. Some larger locomotives have two sets of drive wheels under one boiler. These are articulated locomotives. A 4-6-6-4, which is also called a "Challenger," had four lead wheels, two sets of six drivers each, and four trailing

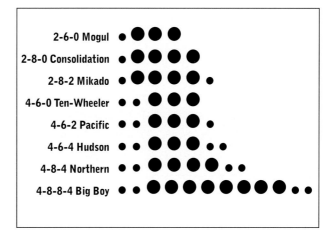

Fig. 6-2 Whyte system of classification (not all wheel arrangements are shown)

Fig. 6-4 Early diesels, such as this EMD FT, were referred to as "covered wagons."

Fig. 6-5 Perhaps one of the finest plastic ready-to-run N scale steam locomotives is the Kato model of the USRA Heavy Mikado. A number of railroads operated these engines in the years between World War I and the end of steam.

Fig. 6-6 This Bachmann 4-8-4 is based on a Santa Fe prototype, despite the "Reading" lettering on the tender. Plastic steam is a good way to build up a roster without the expense of imported brass models.

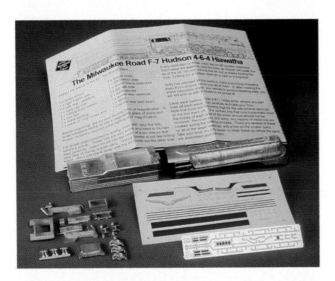

Fig. 6-7 The steam locomotive conversion kits available from GHQ Models fall somewhere between plastic and brass. This particular kit contains all the parts needed to convert a Con-Cor 4-6-4 into a detailed model of the Milwaukee Road's famed *Hiawatha*. Other kits are available for other prototypes and N scale mechanisms.

wheels. Figure 6-2 lists the most common wheel arrangements and the most common nicknames.

Diesel locomotives

The earliest diesel locomotives appeared on the scene as early as the 1920s, but it wasn't until the late 1930s that the "modern" diesel was introduced. The onset of World War II meant the diesel didn't supplant the steam locomotive until the 1950s.

In a diesel locomotive a diesel engine drives an electric generator whose output powers truck-mounted electric motors. Unlike a steam locomotive's operating parts, most of which are visible externally, the mechanical parts of a diesel locomotive are hidden under the sheet-metal body. The typical external parts of a diesel locomotive are shown in figure 6-3.

Diesel locomotive manufacturers offer standard models, which vary little from one railroad to another. This means that one railroad's GP40-2 looks identical to other railroads' GP40-2s, with the possible exception of some minor details such as headlights, horns, and plows.

Early road diesels such as the EMD FT (fig. 6-4) and the Alco FA had full-width carbodies that looked like shorter versions of the manufacturers' six-axle passenger diesels like the E7 and the PA. Alco introduced its RS series (RS stood for "road switcher") in the 1940s, and diesel locomotives haven't looked the same since. The RS, and its direct competitor, EMD's GP series, had long narrow carbodies with walkways on both sides and a short hood on the other side of the full-width cab. The roadswitchers didn't look as sleek as the F units, but their narrow hoods offered better visibility for switching. By the 1960s hood units like the GP9 and the RS-11 had virtually replaced the F units on road freights.

Diesel locomotives enabled railroads to operate longer trains more economically. Because of diesels, railroads needed fewer different locomotive models. Instead of maintaining a fleet of medium, heavy, and light freight steamers, railroads could purchase a number of identical diesels and then assign them to trains as needed. In the 1950s the railfan community hated to see steam go, but management was quite pleased with their diesels.

Modeling steam locomotives

The diversity in the appearance of steam locomotives from one railroad to another is the main reason so few model railroad manufacturers offer steam locomotive models. Unlike diesels, which were and are fairly standardized, there's little chance a manufacturer can offer a steam locomotive that will appeal to virtually every N scale modeler.

Some steam locomotive models are available, of course, ranging in size from the tiny early 4-4-0

Fig. 6-8 Prototype railroads have been turning more and more to the so-called "comfort," or safety, cab that was first introduced in Canada. The result was the first really significant change in the outward appearance of diesels in almost two decades. Kato offers this model of General Electric's Dash 9-44 CW, commonly called a "Dash-9."

Americans to the Big Boys and Challengers that were built toward the end of steam. Kato offers a fine model of a USRA Heavy Mikado (2-8-2) (fig. 6-5), which is perhaps the most detailed plastic ready-to-run steam locomotive available in N scale today.

Since it's based on a USRA prototype, it's an accurate model for locomotives operated by a number of prototype railroads.

Although the major N scale locomotive manufacturers offer only a limited number of types of plastic steam locomotives, like the Santa Fe 4-8-4 from Bachmann which is shown in figure 6-6, quite a number of N scale steam locomotives have been offered over the years in the form of brass imports. Brass models are made overseas (primarily in Korea, although early models were made in Japan) and imported into the country in the form of limited runs. Since brass steamers are basically hand-made, they sell for premium prices.

If you can't afford brass, want a broader selection than plastic, and still want to model steam, you can purchase a conversion kit like those offered by GHQ (fig. 6-7). These kits vary in complexity depending on the prototype. Some, like the Southern Railway 2-8-2 kit, include some new details and boiler fittings. Others, like the Pennsy L-1 and the Northern Pacific W-3, include new boilers, tenders, and a complete set of detail parts. If you take your time and follow the instructions, you'll be rewarded with a detailed steam locomotive that you won't find on everyone else's roster.

Modeling diesel locomotives

N scale modelers have a wide range of diesel models to choose from, unlike the fairly limited selection of steam locomotives. A number of manufacturers offer diesel models in a wide price range. The major manufacturers include Bachmann, Life-Like, Atlas, and Kato. Most N scale diesel have a one-piece plastic body mounted over

Fig. 6-9 With its long nose and classic lines, many railfans and modelers consider the Alco PA-1 to be the ultimate diesel. Several N scale manufacturers offer models of the PA-1. This A-B set (a "B" is a cableless booster) is from Kato.

a split-frame that provides weight for tractive effort.

Like the prototype railroads, you can choose the standard type of locomotives you need for your railroad and purchase the models off the shelf.

The vast majority of N scale diesels on the market today reflect prototypes that were operating from the 1950s through the mid-to-late 1960s. These include four-axle units, such as GP7s, GP9s, RS-3s, and RS-11s. A number of F units are also available, primarily F3s and F7s. In addition, locomotives fairly new in the late 1960s are available, including the GP35, GP40, and SD40. In the last few years, several examples of the newest and most powerful diesels have appeared on the market, including the Bachmann Dash-8, the Kato C44-9W, and the Atlas SD60 and SD60M (fig. 6-8).

It's likely that additional modern diesel locomotives will be offered in model form. This recent popularity of more modern motive power in no way reflects a declining interest in the older diesel locomotives. Those GP9s, F units, E units, and PA-1s (fig. 6-9) continue to serve with pride on many N scale railroads.

In recent years diesel detailing, once almost exclusively limited to HO and larger scales, has become quite popular among N scale modelers. A

Fig. 6-10 An overwhelming number of N scale locomotives are available. If you're just getting started, stick with diesel locomotives. Here are just a few of the many models that will offer years of trouble-free performance.

wide selection of detail parts is available, making it easy to duplicate not only the general type of diesel used by a prototype railroad, but all the details found on the real thing.

With a few hours, some detail parts, a new coat of paint, and some decals you can transform those nicely detailed off-the-shelf models into highly detailed models of the real thing (fig. 6-10).

This fairly recent interest in diesel detailing means that many manufacturers have enhanced their factory-painted locomotives more than ever before. On most top-end N scale locomotives you'll find numbers in the number boards (fig. 6-11). There are even locomotives that are painted and unnumbered, making it easy for those who want to superdetail one locomotive or add different numbers to each unit to develop a fleet of engines.

Selecting power for your layout

In terms of detail, performance, and quality, most of the locomotives you'll find on the hobby dealer's shelves today are way ahead of those offered more than 10 years ago. And while big, modern diesels are becoming popular, smaller locomotives, like Life-Like's SW9/1200, have set new standards for small N scale motive power (fig. 6-12).

As a general rule, the more expensive the locomotive, the more likely you are to be satisfied with the model. Sometimes it's better to have only one or two top-notch locomotives than an entire roster of so-so units. And in general, I recommend that beginners stick to diesel motive power—at least for now. Steamers are much more finicky and seem less tolerant of dirty track and poorly laid track than most diesels. And to be perfectly frank, while there are some nicely detailed, smoothly running N scale steamers out there, in most cases the diesel models are far more reliable than steam locomotives priced at two or three times as much. So think long and hard before you base your railroad on steam power. If you simply must include a steam engine on the layout, consider setting the layout in the steam-to-diesel transition era. This will allow you to build up a roster of reliable diesels now and then turn your attention to the more finicky steam power after you've gained some experience.

In addition to that general advice, you'll also want to consider the following when purchasing a new locomotive for your roster:

• **Is it an appealing model?** The model should capture the overall flavor of the prototype. And, naturally, you should like its looks!

• **Does it fit your theme?** Back in Chapter 2 I discussed the importance of theme in enhancing the realism of the layout. The locomotive should be one found on your prototype during the time

Fig. 6-11 When compared to some of the more recent offerings from Kato and other companies, even a fine model like the Kato GP38-2 (left) looks dated. The latest models, like the Atlas GP40-2 (right), offer closed pilots and have numbers in the number boards.

period you selected to model. If you're freelancing, then you'll want to make sure the locomotive would have been a logical choice for your fictitious railroad.

• **Will it run on your layout?** Long-wheelbased equipment will not operate reliably on sharp curves. You'll want to determine that the locomotive will, indeed, operate around your minimum-radius curve. This information is standard in product reviews published in *Model Railroader* magazine.

• **Is it offered in your favorite roadname?** If it is, then you'll want to obtain the prepainted model. Even if it isn't offered for your favorite road, remember that a model can be repainted and relettered for any railroad. N scale decals and dry transfers are offered by many manufacturers, and most locomotives are sold in undecorated form. Because locomotives are expensive, approach major alterations and complicated paint jobs after learning basic painting and weathering techniques on plastic structures and freight cars first

• **Does the locomotive perform well?** No matter how good a model locomotive looks, if it doesn't run well you'll never be happy with it. If you end up with a fleet of poor runners you may even become so frustrated you give up model railroading entirely. How do you find out how well the model runs? Start by asking the hobby shop

Fig. 6-12 This Life-Like switcher is considered by many to be the best-running and best-looking N scale switcher—ever! Slow speed performance is truly amazing, an especially important consideration in a yard goat.

owner to run the model on a test track for you before you purchase the engine. Run it back and forth a few times, then see how slowly it starts, how much noise it makes, and how good the speed control is. If you can't test the engine before buying it check the reviews of the locomotive in the major magazines. As a general rule, most models that run well off the shelf continue to be good performers, but a poorly running locomotive almost never improves with age.

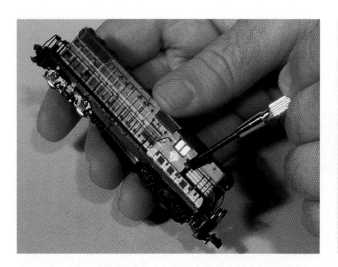

Fig. 6-13 Use a small, flat screwdriver to gently pry the handrails from their mounting holes. Failure to do this can result in broken handrails.

Fig. 6-14 Squeezing the shell will cause the latches to disengage. Very gently twist the shell from side to side while lifting it at the same time. It will come right off the chassis.

Maintenance

In short, most N scale locomotives don't need much in the way of maintenance. The biggest factor that inhibits performance of N scale trains is the same that affects all scales—dirt. Regular cleaning of the track and locomotive wheels will solve the dirt problem. In the chapter on track-laying I mentioned some ways to keep track clean. I clean locomotive wheels by dipping a cotton swab or a pipe cleaner into some ordinary rubbing alcohol and then using this to scrub the wheels. I've found that if the track is kept clean there's little need to clean locomotive wheels more than once or twice a year.

Although most N scale locomotives are reliable, the parts do wear with time and occasionally require replacement. And periodic lubrication and cleaning of the mechanism are also needed. The most common items needing attention are motor brushes and headlight bulbs.

Most locomotives come with a rudimentary set of maintenance instructions. You may be able to obtain the manufacturer's repair sheet for the model from your local hobby shop. If you find your models need maintenance you can either do the work yourself or bring it to the hobby shop. Most shops will perform basic repairs and cleaning for a minimal charge. If you bought the engine at the store, some hobby dealers will perform routine maintenance free of charge.

If you want to do your own maintenance, the first thing you need to do is take the model apart. It's impossible to describe how to disassemble every N scale locomotive, but the following general guidelines should cover the majority of cases.

Most steam locomotive boilers are fastened to the frame by a screw hidden in the smokestack or steam dome. If no screws are visible from above, turn the model over and look directly below the smokestack between the cylinders. In addition to the screws there may be some tab-and-slot fasteners at the rear of the shell, typically on the rear

wall of the cab. Remove the screws and then gently separate the shell from the chassis. By noting the points of resistance you usually can determine the location of additional fasteners. After removing the boiler shell, you can determine the rest of the disassembly sequence by inspection.

When dealing with steam locomotives, disassemble the geared driver sets only when absolutely necessary, since realigning three or four gears is tedious and frustrating work. An improperly reassembled steam locomotive will run poorly, if at all. In extreme cases it's possible to damage an improperly reassembled steamer.

Diesels are much more straightforward. The plastic shell is held in place by tab-and-slot joints along the bottom edges. Figures 6-13 and 6-14 show how to disassemble a typical N scale diesel. Carefully remove the delicate handrails from the holes with a flat screwdriver. Then gently squeeze the body toward the center from both sides and lift the shell from the chassis.

Many model railroaders have strong opinions on the subject of lubricating locomotives. As a general rule, if you're planning to lubricate your locomotives, use only plastic-compatible lubricants, and then apply a small amount. The tip of a toothpick or a small piece of wire make ideal applicators. Why so little? Because a little goes a long way, and over-lubricating a model will cause it to become a magnet for dust and dirt. Before long, the model you've lubricated will no longer work properly.

Some modelers develop a timetable for maintenance, such as lubricating each locomotive after every 100 hours of operation or every six months. I tend to inspect each locomotive and clean and lubricate it once a year. Of course, if a locomotive is acting up, I'll pull it off the layout and take it to the workbench to check it over. In most cases the problem turns out to be dirty wheels, commutators, a loose light board, or a worn brush.

Motor brushes are exposed to more friction than any other part of a model locomotive, so it

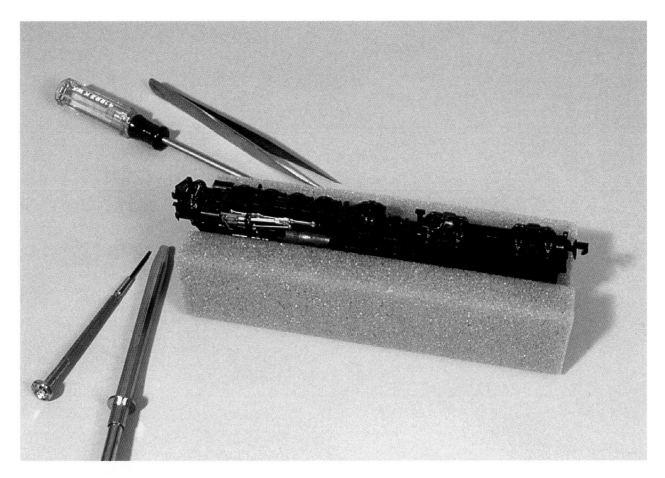

Fig. 6-15 A foam locomotive cradle like this one makes it much easier to work on N scale locomotives without damaging delicate details or scratching the finish.

should come as no surprise that they need the most maintenance. Motor brushes are nothing more than small carbon slugs that provide a sliding electrical connection between the motor terminals and the commutator. The brushes are held in contact with the commutator with a small spring, and this assembly is held in place with a metal plunger called a brush cap. When the motor is running, the brush wears. The spring keeps the brush in contact with the commutator. When the brushes wear down to the point that they are no longer in constant contact with the commutator, the motor suffers momentary loss of electrical contact. This results in erratic operation. If your usually reliable locomotive is starting and stopping, even though the wheels and track are clean, your problem may be worn brushes.

It's a good idea to establish a regular routine for cleaning your motive power fleet. Many modelers I know do locomotive maintenance an hour or two at a time during the summer months—when indoor activities like model railroading traditionally go dormant—saving those long winter months for more involved projects. Others dedicate a certain block of time, say the month of September, to maintenance. All hobby time that month is spent cleaning and maintaining locomotives until everything is finely tuned. Still others always have a locomotive "in the shop" (fig. 6-15) that they clean and repair during odd moments stolen from other modeling projects. In each case the lesson is clear—pay attention to maintenance and you'll be rewarded with a motive power fleet that's ready to go when you are.

CHAPTER SEVEN

CARS

For Freight and Passengers

The evolution and development of railroad cars is a fascinating study. From the earliest cars, which were little more than carts on flanged wheels, to today's stack cars and Superliners, railroads have developed an impressive array of equipment for hauling people, animals, raw materials, and finished goods. For many model railroaders freight and passenger cars are the most interesting part of the hobby. And with good reason, for there is an almost unlimited variety of prototype cars to study and model. And in recent years there has been an explosion in the variety of N scale cars available.

Rolling stock is especially important to N scale modelers, since we need so much of it. Some N scale club layouts run 100- to 150-car trains regularly, the equivalent of those operated by class-one mainline railroads. And home layouts that can accommodate 50- to 75-car trains are fairly common. Even the smallest N scale railroad can consume rolling stock at an astounding rate.

Freight and passenger cars have undergone an evolution just as significant as locomotives over the 170-year history of railroading. In order to choose the most appropriate cars for your layout you must know a little about the development of prototype rolling stock.

Intermodal shipment has continued to grow in popularity among prototype railroads, and many modelers are following suit. This articulated five-car set from Deluxe Innovations can be quite a sight as it winds its way through the landscape carrying a load of containers.

Freight cars

When you stop at a grade crossing and watch a passing freight, you often see examples of many of the unique cars operated by today's railroads. In many cases these cars look like the traditional cars first operated by railroads nearly 100 years ago. Let's run down some basic freight car types and discuss what they're used for:

Boxcars. As the name implies, the boxcar is a essentially a box on wheels. For years any nonperishable product that needed protection from the weather was shipped in boxcars. This included appliances, automobiles (parts and entire automobiles), televisions, and bagged grain. From 1900 through the early 1960s, the 40-foot boxcar dominated the nation's freight car rosters. By the late 1930s the 50-foot cars (fig. 7-1) appeared on the scene in fairly large numbers, although the 40-footer still dominated. Earlier cars had wood sides, often with steel underframes. But by the late 1920s the composite (both wood and steel) and all-steel car had become more common. Composite boxcars, which are properly known as single-sheathed cars, have steel bracing visible on the exterior of the car (fig. 7-2).

Most 40-foot cars were painted in some variant of boxcar red with the railroad's name in white.

But don't be lulled into thinking all boxcars were alike. Several varieties of N scale 40-foot cars, many of which look significantly different, are available. Starting in the late 1940s railroads starting painting their boxcars in more colorful schemes, although the basic boxcar red (or brown) 40-foot car was still the most common. By the 1960s the exterior-post 50-foot boxcar had become the most common style of car, and many of these are still in service today.

Flatcars are perhaps the most basic of freight cars. They are often simply a flat platform used to transport material too large to fit inside a boxcar. Many flatcars are designed for specific use. A flatcar equipped with mounting hitches for a highway trailer is called a piggyback flat. A flatcar with a lowered center section, called a depressed-center flat, is used to transport tall loads such as generators or other large items that would exceed overhead clearances if shipped on a conventional flatcar.

A number of N scale flatcars are available. The biggest problem with plastic flatcars is their light weight. They often have operating problems, especially through curves and turnouts. You can add narrow weights, or even some lead shot poured into weight glue, to the underside of the car.

BUILDING AN INTERMOUNTAIN BOXCAR KIT

InterMountain Railway Co. offers a wide selection of freight cars for N scale modelers, with body styles and paint schemes not available from any other source. And while InterMountain does sell a fair number of cars already assembled, all its cars are also available in kit form. Some N scalers shy away from these kits, thinking they're difficult to build. But with the right tools, some patience, and a willingness to try something new, I'm sure you'll find them easy.

The parts of an InterMountain boxcar kit are shown here.

The only really difficult part of building one of these kits is removing the delicate plastic parts from the sprues without damaging them. (If you do break a part you'll find that extras of the more easily broken parts are included in the kit.) I've tried using a hobby knife, razor blades, and parts nippers like the ones I use to remove parts when building plastic structure kits. I usually managed to break at least a few parts. Then I purchased a set of PBL desprung nippers, and I've never had a problem removing the parts from InterMountain kits since.

The PBL nippers make it easy to cut the parts off the sprue and remove most of the plastic gate, minimizing the need to clean up the parts before assembly.

Also, even though the InterMountain kit is plastic, I find it difficult to bond the parts using liquid plastic, even if I am working with undecorated cars. Instead, I use cyanoacrylate adhesive (CA) to bond the parts together.

Once the parts are off the sprue, I install the underbody details, then place the doors and roof in place. After all the larger parts are together, I add the smaller details like the brake wheel, ladders, and grab irons. All InterMountain kits are assembled in essentially the same way.

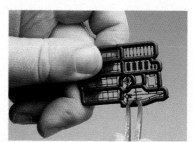

Both the CN 40-foot and the CB&Q 50-foot were built from InterMountain kits.

Another solution is to add a load to the flatcar. White-metal vehicles, such as a tractors, make an interesting load. Another solution to the weight problem is to operate flatcars made from metal, such as the GHQ metal depressed-center flat (fig. 7-3). This easy-to-assemble kit is heavy enough to track reliably.

Gondolas. Add sides to a flatcar and you have a gondola. These cars are used to ship items that need no protection from the elements. Often gondolas are used for steel, scrap iron, and gravel, and in years past they were often used to transport coal.

Because of the rough, even abusive service they see, it's almost impossible to over-weather a gondola model. Gondolas were also originally wood, but because of the rough service, they were some of the first all-steel cars on the railroad.

Micro-Trains, perhaps the biggest name in N scale freight cars, offers several different styles of gondolas in numerous road names. Two typical gons are shown in figure 7-4.

Hoppers. Like gondolas, hopper cars are used to ship products that don't need protection from the elements. Coal is probably the most common item shipped in hoppers, although iron ore and stone are also shipped in these cars. As the name implies, hopper cars have operating doors on the underside of the car that makes it easy to unload their cargo. Hoppers are described by their capacity (50-ton, 70-ton, etc.) although they are also described by the number of hopper bays on the underside of the car. Two-bay (also called twin-pocket) hoppers were used well into the 1950s. Although early examples of three- and four-bay cars were built as early as the late teens, it wasn't until the 1940s that the larger cars become the most dominant (fig. 7-5).

Today hopper cars are typically operated as long unit trains (often 100 cars or more) between coal preparation plants and power plants or export piers where the coal is loaded into ships.

Covered hoppers. Any type of powered or granular commodity that needs protection from the elements is today transported in covered hoppers. Early covered hoppers were nothing more than prototype cars with a roof and hatches added. Since then the covered hopper has evolved into a specialized car. Like their open-top counterparts, covered hoppers are described by the number of bays or by their capacity. Since they are used for specialized transport, many covered hoppers are operated by private owners rather than individual railroads, although a number of railroads continue to operate large fleets of covered hoppers (fig. 7-6).

This means these cars have some of the most colorful paint schemes on the rails today. Among the most colorful are the cars designed for use in Canadian grain service (fig. 7-7).

The cars operated by many independent grain companies are also interesting and unique. And like their open-roofed cousins, today's covered hoppers operate in unit trains, especially in the

Fig. 7-1 The 50-foot boxcar was simply a longer version of the classic 40-foot car. Many 50-foot cars had double doors and hinged ends for automobile loading. This is an Atlas model with double doors and standard ends.

Fig. 7-2 The earliest boxcars were wood. While steel replaced wood in many cars, a large number of single-sheathed cars, like this Roco model, were built between World War I and the 1930s. Composite cars featured steel underframes and braces with wood sheathing. Similar cars were built during World War II in an effort to conserve steel.

Fig. 7-3 GHQ's metal depressed-center flat is an interesting car. Better still, each kit comes with two flatcars and decals for several railroads! I added Micro-Trains trucks and couplers to my model before I painted and decaled it for the New Haven.

midwestern United States and central Canada during the grain harvest season.

In addition to grain, covered hoppers are used to ship plastic pellets, salt, sugar, sand, and carbon black, to name just a few items.

Tank cars. With the possible exception of the intermodal revolution, no other type of car has undergone so much change in recent years as the tank car. As the name implies, the tank car is a tank on wheels used to ship bulk quantities of liquids. In order to avoid contaminating other cargoes, most tank cars are used to ship only one product; so like covered hoppers, these cars are most often operated by private shippers rather than individual railroads.

The earliest tank cars were small and most often painted black (although silver cars could also be seen) (fig. 7-8).

Originally used almost exclusively for bulk oil shipments, today tank cars have grown in size and variety. They haul everything from liquid propane to the kaolin clay slurry used in paper-making. A number of manufacturers offer tank cars. In general the smaller tank cars (like the InterMountain and Micro-Trains 8,000- and 10,000-gallon models) ran from the 1920s through the early 1960s.The more rounded and larger tank cars, like those made by Model Die Casting and Atlas,

came on the scene in large numbers in the 1970s.

Refrigerator cars are used to transport temperature-sensitive cargoes. A typical reefer looks like a boxcar with small, insulated side doors and hatches in the roof. Pacific Fruit Express and the Santa Fe Refrigerator Division were two of the country's largest operators of refrigerator car fleets. Pacific Fruit Express, or PFE, was controlled jointly by the Union Pacific and the Southern Pacific. The SFRD operated as a subsidiary of the Atchison Topeka & Santa Fe. The earliest reefers were nothing more than well-insulated boxcars with bunkers filled with ice in the ends. Since re-icing refrigerator cars was a time- and labor-intensive process, mechanical refrigeration was introduced in the late 1940s. The iced cars were refitted with mechanical cooling units or replaced by the early 1960s.

Steel refrigerator cars, like those shown in fig. 7-9, were common as early as the 1920s, although large numbers of wood-sided produce reefers were operated into the early 1950s. Many railroads rebuilt their wood-sided produce reefers using steel sides, considerably changing their external appearance and extending the cars' useful service lives by many years. Because of the nature of their cargo, refrigerator cars designed for hauling meat products were some of the last

ASSEMBLING A CAST-RESIN BOXCAR

The completed Pennsy double-door is an eye-catching model of a unique prototype. Note the waves in the side of the car, which duplicate the stressed sheet steel on many prototype boxcars.

Some of the most innovative and varied freight cars available to the N scale modeler are limited-run cars made from cast resin. One of the most common manufacturers of N scale resin kits is Fine-N-Scale products, a small company that offers a fairly wide selection of freight car kits and cast-resin loads.

The freight car kits consist of one-piece cast-resin bodies and underframes with etched brass details such as running boards, stirrup steps, and brakewheels. Also included are a set of decals and some weights. Trucks and couplers must be purchased separately, although the models take standard Micro-Trains trucks and couplers readily. Although they may look complicated, there are fewer parts in one of these kits than in many injection-molded plastic boxcar kits. The material used in these

kits is impervious to liquid cement, which means that all the parts must be joined using cyanoacrylate. Perhaps the biggest drawback to the cars for many beginners is the fact that they come unpainted. But they're easy to paint. Just be sure to clean the car thoroughly with soap and water, as the paint will not adhere to the compound used to release the car from the mold.

I painted my Pennsy double-door boxcar with a Polly Scale color called Special Oxide Red, which I find is a close match to the fairly orange red the Pennsy used on these cars. After the model was painted I installed the running boards, stirrup steps, and brakewheel using cyanoacrylate adhesive. These parts were painted with a hand brush after they were on the car.

Then I added the decals to the model, using Microscale Micro-Set to snuggle the decals over the details. An coat of Testor's Dullcote blended the decals into the car side and protected the decals from handling. Finally, I installed a pair of Micro-Trains Bettendorf trucks and placed the finished car in service.

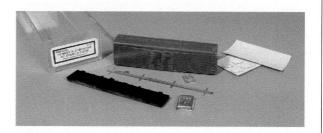

Fig. 7-4 Gondolas like these two Micro-Trains cars are used to transport cargo that needs no protection from the elements.

wood-sided cars on the rails. These cars were adorned with the colorful paint schemes of the various meat packing companies.

Intermodal cars. Unlike the other cars we've discussed, intermodal cars aren't limited to one car type. Intermodal is the term used to describe a type of shipment in which the mode of transportation may change, but the container holding the cargo remains the same. Intermodal shipment uses containers (essentially steel boxes) that can be loaded on a ship, a train, or a trailer so goods can be shipped literally from one point in the world to another without being unloaded and then reloaded one or more times. The cost savings to shippers and consignees alike is tremendous. Railroads have taken full advantage of intermodal shipment in the last couple of decades. Starting with piggyback shipment in the 1930s and 40s, railroads have developed an impressive array of specialized intermodal equipment including spine cars, specialized flatcars, well cars, and double-stack cars. In addition to an impressive array of containers, many styles and types of cars are available, such as the Gunderson articulated well car from Deluxe Innovations. And nothing looks better behind one of those big Dash-9s than a long string of stack cars.

Intermodal is a significant development that you'll want to learn more about if you're interested in modeling the period from 1960 through the present day. And the more recent your era, the more you'll want to know about intermodal. But it's a topic far more complex than I can cover in detail here. For an excellent introduction to intermodal I highly recommend Jeff Wilson's book *The Model Railroader's Guide to Intermodal Equipment and Operation*, from Kalmbach Publishing Co.

Cabooses. Another significant change in recent years is the virtual elimination of the caboose. Once a standard sight on the rear of every freight train, reduced crews and technological innovations mean that the caboose has been replaced by the Flashing Rear End Train Device, or FRED.

Even though you don't see it in the real world much anymore, the caboose hasn't lost its appeal to modelers.

If you're modeling the years before 1990 or so you'll want to include a number of cabooses on your layout. Like steam locomotives cabooses tended to differ from railroad to railroad. For that reason many modelers opt to use detailed brass cabooses so they have cars accurate for their prototype.

If the budget doesn't allow for brass imports you'll find a wide array of plastic cars are available (fig. 7-10).

Fig. 7-5 Hopper cars can unload cargo by opening the bottom (hopper) doors. Most hoppers were, and are, used for coal shipments. This car is a Model Die Casting car based on a 70-ton design typical of those used between the late 1940s and into the 1970s.

Fig. 7-6 Like their open-top cousins, covered hoppers can also be unloaded using gravity. These two Micro-Trains cars feature operating roof hatches.

Fig. 7-7 The Canadian government built large numbers of cylindrical covered hoppers for grain service starting in the early 1970s. The prototype cars were painted in some colorful schemes as well as standard railroad livery. These are InterMountain kits.

Fig. 7-8 This model of an 8,000-gallon tank car by InterMountain is typical of those operated in the years before, during, and after World War II.

Fig. 7-9 A typical refrigerator car had ice bunkers in the ends with roof hatches and small insulated doors on the sides. These Santa Fe reefers featured a system map on one side and promotions for the railroad's famous name trains on the other. Both these cars are InterMountain kits.

Although they may not match your specific prototype, often all that's needed is a coat of paint and some decals to come pretty close. Some etched-brass and resin kits are also available that let you acquire specific prototype models at near plastic prices.

Other types. In addition to the significant car types mentioned here others include stock cars, milk cars, autoracks, and other cars designed for transporting specific cargoes. There are also subclasses of some of the common types of cars listed above, such as insulated boxcars and tank cars. All play a key role in transporting goods where they're needed. And all can contribute to the realism of your N scale railroad (fig. 7-11).

Selecting freight cars

The explosion in N scale freight cars in recent years makes it possible for N scale modelers to acquire examples of virtually every type of freight car built for the prototype over the last 70 years. Modeling older railroads is hampered by a limited selection of rolling stock. When we discussed locomotives I advised sticking with the steam-to-diesel transition era or later because of equipment reliability and selection. The same holds true for freight cars. It's no accident that the widest selection of freight cars covers the time period 1950 through the present.

Selecting the appropriate freight cars for your layout is a tough task all modelers face. Some take it very seriously, narrowing their focus to a specific month, day, or year. Others take a broader approach. The most important thing is to select freight cars that fit in with the layout's era. You'll also want to select cars that reflect the traffic in the area you're modeling. A string of Chesapeake & Ohio hopper cars would be out of place in the

Fig. 7-10 If the budget doesn't allow for brass, you can obtain several nice plastic caboose models. The wood car on the right (Micro-Trains) is an earlier era, while the wide-cupola Atlas Maine Central car reflects some of the last cabooses built.

California desert. Likewise, long strings of yellow reefers would look odd on a layout that featured a coal branch operation in the Appalachians.

When choosing cars appropriate for the era, start by looking at the box. Often the box contains information on when the prototype cars were built and used. As a general rule, cars painted in darker shades such as boxcar red, brown, and black reflect the 1950s and earlier. More brightly colored cars are typical of the 1960s and later. Also, as a general rule, freight cars have grown larger over the years. The bigger the car, the later the era.

Finally, I believe the higher the percentage of "typical" cars, the larger the layout looks. If every car is a colorful rolling billboard, each car may become too familiar. A sea of nearly identical red boxcars or black hoppers, no matter what road name, can make the car fleet, and therefore the whole railroad, look much larger. Studying photos of your favorite prototype will also provide some hint of how to develop a realistic car fleet for your layout.

Passenger cars

Passenger cars can be colorful and interesting and provide a nice diversion from freight cars. Unfortunately, most model railroaders don't include much passenger traffic on their layouts. After all, passenger trains were *the* way to travel before airliners and interstate highways came along.

On May 1, 1971, most of the long-distance passenger rail travel in the United States was turned over to the National Rail Passenger Corp., which is more commonly known as Amtrak. Amtrak was formed by an act of Congress to save intercity passenger service, which the railroads were eager to cancel because of heavy operating losses. Although it's had some ups and downs over the years,

Amtrak is a success story, and today it operates an efficient system of trains on selected routes.

In the golden era of passenger rail travel, essentially the years prior to 1960, passenger trains of the major railroads were a source of pride and intense competition. The first-class trains wore matching paint schemes and featured every conceivable luxury.

Since they were the pride of the operating railroads, passenger trains were well maintained. They were assigned the newest and fastest power on the railroad and given priority over every other train on the line. These trains carried sleeping cars, dining cars, lounge cars, and observation cars. Some carried priority mail in specially decorated baggage-mail or Railway Post Office cars. Many were exclusive first-class trains, with no coaches in the consist.

The basic types of passenger cars include:

Coaches. These cars provide routine accommodations for short trips, typically one or two days.

Sleepers. Depending on the particular car, sleepers offer a combination of roomettes, bedrooms,

Fig. 7-11 Freight cars haul everything from apples to zinc. Here are just a few of the hundreds of N scale freight cars offered. Collect cars based on paint schemes and road names, or select cars in a more systematic way to support the traffic your railroad hauls. Either way, there's a wide selection.

Fig. 7-12 These Rivarossi heavyweight passenger cars, painted and lettered for the Canadian National, are typical of those available to N scale modelers.

suites, or in some cases simply beds. The original sleeping cars were designed in the mid-1800s, and the most famous builder was the Pullman Company. Most sleepers were operated by the Pullman Company as late as the 1950s.

Dining cars were rolling restaurants that offered a selection of dishes reflecting the region served by the railroad.

Café or lounge cars were similar in many ways to dining cars, although the kitchens were usually smaller. Typically these cars offered snacks and lighter, less formal, dining than that found in the diner.

Observation cars featured large windows so patrons could enjoy the landscape. Some observation cars had rounded ends and were placed at the rear of the train. Other observation cars featured glass-roofed domes, which provided truly panoramic views of the landscape.

Parlor cars tended to be more common on eastern railroads because of the shorter runs. They were essentially first-class coaches, often with luxurious individual swiveling seats and large windows. Some trains offered all-parlor service. The New Haven Railroad's *Merchants Limited* between New York City and Boston is perhaps the most famous parlor train.

Although they didn't haul passengers directly, other cars were typical on passenger trains, including Railway Post Office cars, where mail was sorted by clerks while the train was moving; bulk-mail storage cars, which transported already sorted mail; and baggage cars, which "Agency (REA), the

predecessor of today's parcel services, had a large fleet of express cars that were common sights in the nation's passenger trains for many years. Loss of this revenue, especially the government mail contracts, spelled the beginning of the end for many passenger trains. In some cases the U. S. Mail, which once provided the revenue to keep otherwise unprofitable passenger trains in the black, has returned to the rails, and it's not unusual to see several bulk storage cars of mail and express packages on the tail end of today's long-distance passenger trains operated by Amtrak.

Selecting passenger cars

If you want to ensure that your passenger equipment is completely authentic, you'll have to do some research. Most N scale passenger cars are based on one railroad's distinctive passenger equipment. They are offered in a variety of popular paint schemes of other railroads that may have never operated anything even similar in appearance. If you're unsure of the prototype for a passenger car, try to find the review of the car in model railroad magazines; the reviewer should specify the prototype.

As with freight cars, the earliest passenger cars were built of wood. Vestibules, which are closed walkways between two cars, came into use in the 1880s. The first all-steel passenger cars were built in the early 1900s, and heavyweight (80- to 90-ton) cars were the standard from the early teens through the 1930s. The Chicago, Burlington & Quincy's *Pioneer Zephyr* ushered in the streamlined

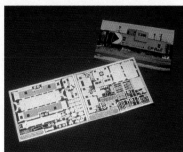

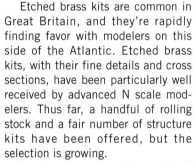

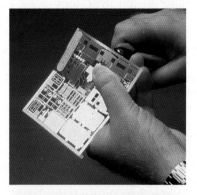

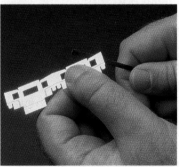

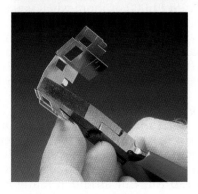

Buzz Lenander built this Athabaska Scale Models N scale caboose from an etched brass kit. Model and photo by Buzz Lenander, courtesy of Athabaska Scale Models.

Etched brass kits are common in Great Britain, and they're rapidly finding favor with modelers on this side of the Atlantic. Etched brass kits, with their fine details and cross sections, have been particularly well received by advanced N scale modelers. Thus far, a handful of rolling stock and a fair number of structure kits have been offered, but the selection is growing.

As the name implies, etched brass kits consist flat sheets of brass, called frets, that have been chemically etched to remove unwanted material. Highly detailed sections are all that remains; they include etched fold lines to aid in assembling the car.

The completed Athabaska Scale Models caboose shown here is a detailed replica of a Canadian Pacific wide-cupola car. The photos and captions show some of the tools and offer a few tips on assembling one of these highly detailed models. Although the parts can be soldered together, it's easier to join the parts together using cyanoacrylate.

Be sure to keep the fret as flat as possible to prevent accidentally bending the parts.

You probably already own many of the tools needed to build an etched brass kit. Most important is a square to assist in bending the parts to a 90 degree angle. A good pair of cutters is also essential for removing

the delicate parts from the fret. I'd also recommend you have a good set of jeweler's files and some flat-nosed pliers.

Be sure to read the directions completely before starting assembly. The vast majority of the parts bend with the guides on the inside of the car, but there are a few parts that bend "inside out." It's important to identify these to avoid bending a part the wrong way, since it's impossible to bend a part back without breaking it.

Use the nippers to cut the parts from the fret as you need them. Trimming close to the part will minimize the time required for filing.

Then use jeweler's files to remove any traces of flash on the parts. Work slowly and carefully and pause to check your work frequently.

Flat-tipped pliers make it easy to bend the parts to shape. Line the nose of the pliers along the fold line and then use your other hand to gently bend the part to the approximate angle. Using the pliers prevents bending the part more than 90 degrees. For smaller areas use the pliers to cover the part to be bent and then bend it to shape with the pliers.

Once the parts have been bent to the proper shape, you can install the parts on the car using cyanoacrylate. Atlas caboose trucks are ideal, and several manufacturers offer appropriate paint and lettering.

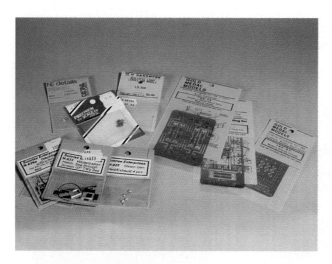

Fig. 7-13 Lately, a tremendous number of detail parts have become available for N scale locomotives and rolling stock. Availability of these parts have made N, long a bastion of "ready-to-run" trains, into a true "modeler's" scale.

Fig. 7-14 These two cars are identical, except that one has been weathered using washes of dilute black paint and some powdered chalk. Weathering is the simplest, and cheapest, way to make your models look more realistic.

era in 1934. Welded stainless-steel components replaced the earlier riveted steel cars, reducing the weight per car to 60 tons or so. The newer stainless cars were also a perfect complement to the new-fangled diesel locomotives then coming into vogue, and the streamlined era was born.

Although the first-class trains have always received the newest and best equipment, railroads were reluctant to scrap older cars. Typically the earlier equipment was bumped into secondary mainline and branchline service as newer equipment became available for the name trains. Wooden passenger cars remained in service until after World War II, and heavyweight sleeping cars, many with air-conditioning added, operated in the Pullman fleet through the 1960s. And heavyweight coaches, diners, and head-end cars were used right up to the Amtrak era.

Modeling passenger cars

Despite the variety of prototype passenger cars, there isn't such a wide selection of N scale passenger equipment, but the situation is looking up. For many years all we had to choose from was a limited selection of body styles, like those shown in fig. 7-12, with different paint schemes. Of course there were brass imports, but a train can easily cost a $1,000 or more when you set out to equip it with a fleet of detailed brass cars.

Recently the introduction of American Limited passenger car core kits has created the opportunity for an extensive selection of accurate passenger cars at a reasonable cost.

Detailing and weathering

Read through some articles in the model railroad magazines and you may get the impression that every model on the layout has to be detailed to the nth degree. Nothing could be further from the truth. But although many N scale cars look pretty good right out of the box, I'd encourage you

to try to add some additional details to a few cars. A wide range of freight and passenger car detail parts is available, with the selection growing regularly (fig. 7-13).

Although adding individual details to an individual car is easy and fun, detailing a fleet of cars large enough to equip even a modest home layout can be a daunting task. Perhaps the easiest way to increase the realism of any car fleet is to weather the rolling stock.

Some N scale modelers I've met refuse to weather their cars and locomotives. They have their reasons, and I'll admit there are a few cars that I've obtained over the years that I find so colorful and interesting that I don't weather them. Instead of putting those conversation pieces on the layout I display them on shelves in the layout room. Every piece of rolling stock that goes onto the layout gets at least a little weathering.

Weathering imparts that sense of mass that's just not there with fresh out-of-the box N scale rolling stock. The difference between an unweathered and weathered car is truly startling (fig. 7-14). If the difference is that significant for one car, imagine what weathering the entire car fleet can do for your the realism of the layout!

Keep 'em rolling

Whether you decide to build rolling stock that's 100 percent realistic, or leave your cars pristine, or weather them so much they look like they're on their last miles, you'll always want your cars to be in good running condition. Most ready-to-run N scale rolling stock is virtually maintenance-free, and most kits can be built into reliably operating cars with a little care. Here are a few of the key elements in trouble-free operation and the type of attention they require:

Wheels. An accumulation of crud can build up on the wheel treads, especially if the track is dirty. Remove it with the same cleaning solvent used to

Right out of the box most N scale freight cars look pretty good, but sometimes the free-standing details such as boxcar running boards and tank car grab irons are oversized. Often these problems are on older cars, or those intended for the toy hobby market. Most plastic cars that are acceptable out of the box can be easily improved using commercial parts and some simple techniques.

Gold Metal Models offers a detail set for modern boxcars that can be used on a number of different kits. In this case I'm detailing a Model Die Casting 50-foot modern boxcar.

I painted the underframe Grimy Black and set it aside to dry. Next, I used a brush to paint the roof of the car Polly Scale Flat Aluminum. Most modern freight cars have unpainted roofs, so this really improved the model with very little effort.

After the roof dried I cut away the plastic stirrup steps and then used a pin vise to drill no. 78 holes for the new brass parts. I also trimmed away the plastic platform on the ends of the car and filled the oversized brakewheel hole with some 1/16" Evergreen plastic rod.

After I installed the Gold Metal Detail parts with cyanoacrylate, I added some weathering to the roof and used a small brush to paint the detail parts to match the car. Gold Metal Models kits are a great way to detail inexpensive rolling stock without having to ruin a hard-to-replicate factory paint job. This is an easy way to create a detailed rolling stock roster for any N scale layout.

clean the track. Soaking a piece of a cotton cloth in the solvent and then gently pushing the car back and forth across it will remove most of the crud. Be sure to wipe the wheels on a dry cloth to remove any residue completely before placing the car back in service.

Wheel gauge. N scale wheelsets occasionally get out of gauge and cause derailments. If a particular car gives you trouble, check the wheel gauge. Micro-Trains makes a handy gauge, the MT-1055, for this, or you can use an NMRA standards gauge.

If I find a wheel out of gauge I never try to regauge the axle, I simply replace the axle with a new one. Frankly, this is required so infrequently that messing around with regauging wheels just isn't worth my hobby time.

Bolster pins. These can be a source of frustration, since an improperly installed bolster pin can cause the truck to sit unevenly. At best this causes the car to tilt at a funny angle. At worst the truck will fall off the car, causing quite a derailment. Micro-Trains sells replacement bolster pins of different styles, depending on the model manufacturer of the car that's experiencing problems. Or you can simply drill and tap a hole and mount the trucks with screws.

CHAPTER EIGHT

COUPLERS

Two types of couplers, each with numerous variations, have been used by prototype railroads in North America—the link-and-pin type, and the knuckle type.

The link-and-pin was used from the earliest railroads through the end of the 19th century. Cars were coupled together by hand. A trainman stood between two cars (one moving and one stationary) and dropped a pin at the second the link was in the proper position. This was obviously very dangerous, and many railroad workers were seriously injured or killed outright when the pin didn't drop correctly and they were caught between the two cars.

In the 1880s railroads started converting to the knuckle-type automatic coupler invented by Eli Janney. Slight variations have been made to the coupler over the years, but the same basic design remains in use today. With it, both coupling and uncoupling can be done fairly safely. Couplers mate automatically. Uncoupling is accomplished using a lever that disengages the pin while the railroad worker is standing beside the car, not between two cars.

N scale couplers

Coupling and uncoupling N scale cars together is not dangerous, but it can be frustrating. There are several types of N scale couplers on the market: the Rapido, the Micro-Trains Magne-Matic automatic knuckle coupler, and

several one-piece knuckle couplers such as those made by InterMountain and Red Caboose.

Rapido couplers are the most common type of N scale coupler on a great deal of ready-to-run equipment, including most N scale locomotives (fig. 8-1).

Rapido couplers are simple in design and operation. The couplers have a pointed front edge and are free to pivot up and down. When two couplers meet, one coupler rides up over the other and falls into place, coupling the cars together.

There are two ways to uncouple cars equipped with Rapido couplers. You can lift one end of one car in the air, a difficult arrangement, since you often have to replace the car on the track. It's easy to derail the car you've uncoupled or any around it. There are automatic uncoupling ramps available for Rapido couplers. These use a small plunger with a shoe on top to push the pin below the coupler up, disengaging the coupler. Cars to be uncoupled must be placed directly over the ramp.

Although some N scale modelers like them, I personally dislike Rapido couplers. Even though they may work fine, they're oversized and look nothing like real couplers. In short, they detract from the appearance of the cars and locomotives.

Solid-knuckle couplers. These couplers, which are made by InterMountain and Red Caboose, look much more like prototype couplers (fig. 8-2).

Lately, much N scale rolling stock is coming factory-equipped with knuckle couplers, such as the popular line made by Micro-Trains. Still, you'll need to know how convert some older locomotives and cars. Micro-Trains offers a tremendous assortment of coupler conversion kits.

Fig. 8-1 Earlier N scale diesels, such as this Atlas RS-11, had large unprototypical openings in the pilot to accommodate sharp curves and the oversized Rapido coupler.

Fig. 8-2 Solid knuckle couplers are included with InterMountain's own N scale freight cars, like the Alberta grain hopper, and those of some other manufacturers, including the DeLuxe Innovations 40-foot boxcar.

They couple automatically when two cars are pushed together. They can be uncoupled either by lifting one end of one car up, or by using a small uncoupling tool, such as that sold by Rix Products, or even a small screwdriver to twist the knuckles away from one another, thus disengaging the couplers. This takes some practice, but it can be done.

Many modelers, even those who prefer Micro-Trains Magne-Matic couplers for their freight cars and locomotives, use solid knuckle couplers for passenger cars and multiunit locomotive sets. Since these couplers aren't automatic, they're much less likely to accidentally uncouple than any other style of coupler.

Micro-Trains couplers. If you've seen or purchased any Micro-Trains rolling stock, then you've noticed that the couplers look different from the larger Rapido-style couplers. These couplers, called Micro-Trains Magne-Matics, look and operate more

CONVERTING TO MICRO-TRAINS COUPLERS

Two Atlas Geeps: before, left, with a Rapido coupler, and after installation of Micro-Trains couplers.

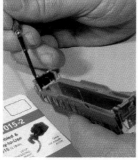

Most N scale locomotives come equipped with Rapido couplers, meaning that your first Micro-Trains installation will be on a diesel locomotive. Earlier diesels, such as the Atlas RS-11 shown in fig. 8-1, had open pilots to allow room for the coupler and truck to swing on tight curves. To convert these locomotives to Micro-Trains couplers, you'll have to purchase a conversion kit specifically for your locomotive. For example, the Micro-Trains 1150 is for the Atlas RS-11. The conversion kit comes with detailed installation instructions and, more important, a special pilot that fills the gap required by the Rapido coupler.

Most of the newer N scale locomotives, such as the GP9 shown here, have closed pilots with a small opening for the couplers. It's easy to convert these locomotives to Micro-Trains using a preassembled coupler, in this case the 1015-2.

Start by removing the shell from the chassis. Then use a small screwdriver to remove the clip holding the coupler in place.

Discard the Rapido coupler and small brass strap (which acts as a spring), but retain the clip.

Now slide the Micro-Trains coupler into the opening in the pilot. It may be necessary to file any burrs or obstructions from the coupler box or pilot opening. The coupler should slide for a snug fit. Reinsert the clip to hold the coupler securely in place.

Fig. 8-3 These two cars from Fine N-Scale (left) and InterMountain (right) have been equipped with Micro-Trains Magne-Matic couplers.

Fig. 8-4 Uncoupling ramps

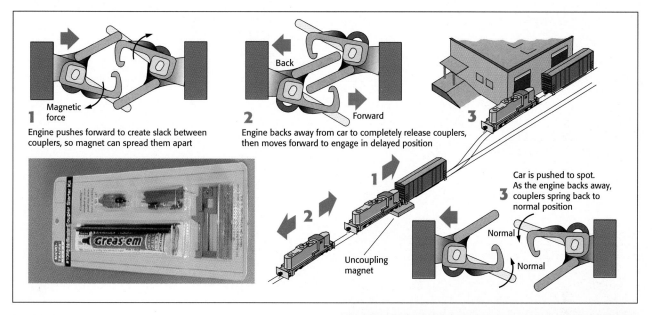

1 Magnetic force
Engine pushes forward to create slack between couplers, so magnet can spread them apart

2 Back / Forward
Engine backs away from car to completely release couplers, then moves forward to engage in delayed position

3 Car is pushed to spot. As the engine backs away, couplers spring back to normal position

Uncoupling magnet

Normal / Normal

Fig. 8-5 Delayed-action uncoupling with micro-trains couplers

Fig. 8-6 (Photo inset) The Coupler Starter Kit contains everything you need to install and check Micro-Trains couplers.

like the real thing and are therefore the choice of most serious N scalers (fig. 8-3).

The coupler, including the shank, is split into two horizontal layers: The knuckle is attached to the top half and the remainder of the coupler head is attached to the lower half of the shank. The couplers open and close with a scissors action. When two cars are pushed together, the knuckles spread apart and then close together to engage.

The real magic of these couplers is the way they uncouple. A small piece of wire is installed on each coupler and uncoupling is accomplished using a special uncoupling ramp (fig. 8-4), which is nothing more then a magnet. Figure 8-5 shows more details on how these couplers couple and uncouple. Incidentally, you can couple together cars equipped with Micro-Trains couplers and those equipped with solid couplers. Obviously, the magnetic uncoupling feature only works when you're uncoupling two Micro-Trains-equipped cars.

Fig. 8-7 You can check the height of your Micro-Trains couplers using the 1055 height gauge. Make sure the trip pins on each car are the correct height above the rail, or they could catch on something, causing a derailment.

Micro-Trains offers a vast line of couplers, trucks, wheels, and accessories. I recommend that you obtain one of its Coupler Starter Kits (fig. 8-6), which includes several types of Micro-Trains couplers, some dry lubricant, and a test gauge (fig. 8-7).

Installing Micro-Trains couplers is fairly straightforward, but always be sure to read the instructions and use the recommended coupler for the particular installation. Properly installed Micro-Trains couplers will add greatly to your enjoyment of N scale railroading.

CHAPTER NINE

BUILDINGS

Models That Don't Roll

It's likely the first N scale model you'll build will be a building, or structure, kit. Structures can add a great deal of interest and individuality to any model railroad, and since they provide visual clues to the purpose of your railroad, they are a critical part of the scene.

Building kits are a great way to get started in model building for several reasons. Their familiar components makes them a little less intimidating than rolling stock for a beginning modeler. They are also large enough, even in N scale, to be worked on easily, and they come in a wide variety of shapes and sizes.

A large number of N scale buildings are also offered ready-assembled. So if kit assembly and modification don't appeal to you, you'll find these buildings will meet your needs, especially if you paint and weather them to make them look unique. I'll show you how to do that a little later in this chapter. For now, let's explore the different types of buildings on and around the railroad and the various types of kits that are available in N scale.

Structures say a great deal about the area and era modeled on a layout. On Bill Denton's Kingsbury Branch, the structures are the scenery. Bill kitbashed the E. B. Millar Co. building by combining several Model Power Baldwin Locomotive Works kits. Bill Denton

Fig. 9-1 **Here's a small sampling, a few of the hundreds of N scale structure kits that are available.**

Types of structures

Almost any structure that exists in the real world can be included on a model railroad layout. But, like everything else, the space available on the layout is limited, so it's important to choose structures carefully. Model railroad structures can be divided into three broad classifications: right-of-way structures, trackside structures, and nonrailroad structures.

Right-of-way structures are those that form an integral part of the railroad and include bridges, trestles, tunnel portals, culverts, turntables, and signal bridges. Including these structures will increase the realism and the visual interest of the layout. Anything you can place on the layout that adds to the apparent length of the train's journey will make the layout seem larger since the eye will naturally be drawn to those places and linger there.

Trackside structures are as important as right-of-way structures and are in many ways the most popular. Trackside structures support the railroad's purpose of transporting goods and people from one place to another. Railroad-owned structures include passenger stations, freight houses, servicing facilities like roundhouses and coaling towers, piggyback ramps, and interlocking and signal towers. Customer-owned trackside structures include any and all industries with a railroad siding, including factories, mills, creameries, and intermodal yards, to name just a few.

Many trackside structures are available as kits, but again, if you want to build your own you'll find that plans for such buildings are published

regularly. Or you can find a likely building in your home town and construct it in miniature.

Nonrailroad structures, although not as important to the operation of the layout as the two other types, are also important and should be included to enhance the realism of the scene. Even if the layout is small you should include at least a small sampling of the stores, houses, service stations, schools, and other buildings to show that the railroad serves communities.

Three ways to get the structures you want

Model railroaders have three basic ways to acquire buildings for their layouts in addition to the pre-assembled buildings mentioned earlier. You can construct building kits "stock," "kitbashed," or "scratchbuilt."

Building stock means, just as the name implies, taking a structure kit and assembling it as the manufacturer intended. In many cases you'll find a coat of flat model paint, or at least some flat clear coating like Testor's Dullcote, will enhance the appearance of any building, even a common structure like the Bachmann farmhouse.

But building a kit as the manufacturer intends often means you end up with a structure that's also seen on hundreds, if not thousands, of other layouts. For generic buildings, this is fine, but to have a unique building it's often worth the trouble to kitbash or scratchbuild that special structure.

Kitbashing may sound like the desperate act of a frustrated modeler, but the term implies a much gentler approach than the name may indicate at first. Art Curren, a well-known modeler who popularized the idea, prefers to call it "kit-mingling," since you really have to coax the finished model together. No matter what it's called, the basic process is the same: start with one or several kits, often from different manufacturers, and combine various parts in order to create a unique building that doesn't look like any of its component parts. You can also combine several versions of the same kit to create a building that's larger than the original.

Scratchbuilding. If you just can't find a kit or components to build a kitbashed model of a building you've just got to have on the layout you'll have to resort to scratchbuilding. As the name implies, that means taking some raw material and building a model without the benefit of the kit. This may seem scary at first, but it does not have to be. Despite its small size, scratchbuilding in N scale is fairly easy, since the large number of details that have to be included for a model to look "right" in the larger scales just aren't that visible on an N scale building. And a scratchbuilt building will often become the centerpiece of the scene.

Kit assembly tips

Visit a well-stocked N scale hobby shop and you'll be overwhelmed by the variety of structure kits (fig. 9-1).

You'll find that kits are offered in several materials, each with its own characteristics. The most common materials for N scale structures are plastic, resin, and wood. In addition, etched brass structure kits are also becoming popular. Don't let the material the kit is made from scare you; simply choose a building that looks appealing and interesting.

Since your first N scale kit will most likely be a plastic building, let's start with some tips for assembling and finishing a typical structure.

Remove the parts from the box and spread them out in front of you (fig. 9-2).

Take a few moments to review the instructions and look at the parts to familiarize yourself with the various subassemblies and components.

When you're ready to begin be sure to cut the parts from the sprues. Don't twist or break them off. (The sprue is the feeder hole through which the plastic is pumped to reach the casting cavities during manufacturing.)

Study the relationship of the various parts. In most kits, the part is identified by a letter or code on the inside edge as an assembly guide.

Assemble plastic models with plastic liquid styrene cement. Don't use tube gel cements—they are next to impossible to control and will only lead to a marred, damaged model. It's important to apply the cement with a small paintbrush. Align the two parts to be joined and dab a brushload of cement at the top of the joint. Figure 9-3 shows how to use a square to ensure a strong, square corner joint. Capillary action will pull the cement along the edge of the joint, producing a firm bond.

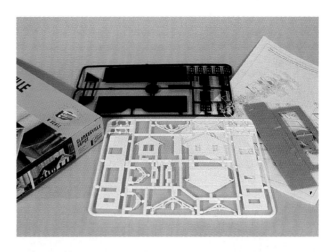

Fig. 9-2 **Lay out the various parts of the kit. Review the instructions and familiarize yourself with the parts and assembly sequence.**

Fig. 9-3 **Use a square to keep the walls perpendicular and apply a dab of a liquid cement to the top of the corner with a small brush. The cement runs down the joint, bonding the parts together. Allow the cement to dry before touching that area of the model or moving the part. It should set up fairly quickly.**

Just be careful your fingers don't get too close to the liquid cement—the plastic will soften enough to take a fingerprint, marring your model.

Wooden structure kits

For many years wooden structure kits were the province of the experienced modeler. Not only did they include more pieces than a comparable plastic kit, they required the model builder to cut out the openings for the doors and windows and in some cases form the walls from pieces of sheet siding. But lately a new range of wooden structure kits have made it easy for even beginning modelers to build a good-looking wood structure without the need for precise cutting or measuring. These newer kits are made by assembling laser-cut walls, roofs, and other components (fig. 9-4). The precise

I've always had a thing for old country stores with their assortment of advertisements and wide selection of merchandise. Many of the ones I've visited stock everything "a mile wide and an inch deep." So when American Model Builders released its N scale laser kit for the Corydon General Store and Post Office I couldn't resist building one. And who knows, perhaps we can add a little character along the way.

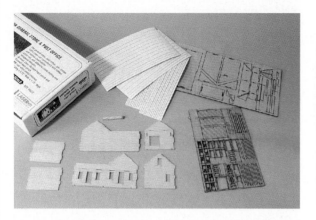

Fig 1 Here's what you'll find when you open the box. American Model Builders Corydon General Store kit is typical of many laser-cut wood kits.

Fig. 2 After interlocking two of the walls together I used the square to keep them steady and then applied a small amount of yellow glue to the inside corner with a toothpick.

Fig. 3 After the walls dried I used a hobby knife to carefully pry up some of the clapboards. I also cut some of the bottom edges of the clapboards. It's easy to overdo this, so take it easy with this step.

Fig. 4 I added the roof, which also includes interlocked tabs, and painted the building with a thin coat of Polly Scale Aged White.

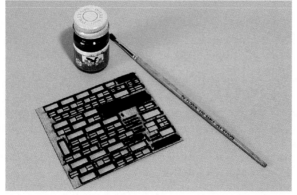

Fig. 5 The windows, doors, and trim have peel-and-stick backing that sticks in place without glue. I paint the trim pieces and windows while everything is in one piece. I applied a coat of Polly Scale Maine Central Pine Green with a brush.

Fig. 6 The signs (from Microscale and Blair Line) and the weathered siding give this model a great deal of character.

Fig. 9-4 **Laser-cut wood kits make it possible for beginners and veterans alike to have detailed wood structures. These are two of the many kits available from American Model Builders. Other companies also offer laser kits.**

cutting action of the laser takes all the guesswork, and much of the hard work, out of assembly.

American Model Builders was one of the first and is currently the biggest manufacturer of laser-cut kits for N scale. But the techniques for assembly and painting apply to any laser kit from any manufacturer.

To assemble a laser-cut kit you'll need many of the same tools required for a plastic kit, although you can forego the sprue cutters and the liquid styrene cement. To assemble a wood kit use yellow carpenter's glue or a high-quality white glue. I pour a small amount of glue onto a small piece of scrap material and then use a toothpick to apply the glue to the model. It's also a good idea to have a small machinist's square to be sure the walls are truly square. In the Corydon General Store and many other laser kits, the walls and roof components are keyed (notched), making it impossible to assemble the model incorrectly.

Some laser-cut buildings use peel-and-stick assembly. The most common uses for peel-and-stick are the window and door assemblies and the roof material. The photos show how to assemble the peel-and-stick windows. Just be sure everything is lined up properly before you stick things in place—it's very difficult to pry the pieces apart without breaking them.

Just as with plastic kits, it's a good idea to paint the window and doors before installing them, especially if you plan to have the trim in a contrasting color.

Two other materials, resin and etched brass, have become more popular for structures in the

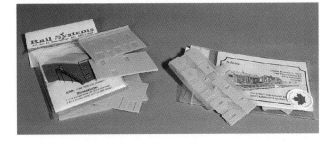

Fig. 9-5 **Although early N scale resin kits consisted of a single piece, more conventional kits, like these from Sylvan Scale Models and Rail Systems, are becoming more popular.**

past few years and their use will very likely continue to grow as more N scalers become familiar with them. Resin buildings are available as one-piece castings with the doors, windows, and details all cast in place; or they can be similar to plastic and wood kits, with individual walls and roof components (fig. 9-5).

The two most important things to remember about resin kits are: make sure the parts are clean, or paint won't adhere to the resin; and use cyano-acrylate adhesive (CA) to assemble the kit.

Etched-brass kits, like the Showcase Miniatures' gas station (fig. 9-6), are among the most finely detailed N scale structures.

They are also more expensive than plastic or wood kits. Some of the more elaborate brass kits require the modeler to apply several layers to a single base piece. This is helpful when the kit is for a Victorian house, for example, that calls for several colors of trim. Most brass kits require

Fig. 9-6 **Etched brass kits offer fine window cross sections that just aren't possible with other materials. The Showcase Miniature's garage kit folds up into a nicely detailed model.**

bending along etched guidelines. In some cases, reverse folds are required. It's always a good idea to carefully read the kit instructions when dealing with brass kits.

Individualizing your structures

You can look upon a structure kit in one of two ways: it's a collection of parts that can be assembled into a particular model; or it's a collection of walls, roofs, windows, doors, chimneys, and so on. You can build the model straight from the box or use your imagination to combine all the various components from one or more kits to create a unique building.

Kitbashing will help get rid of the "I've seen that building before" syndrome that's so common with straight-from-the box kit buildings. Does that mean you shouldn't use any kit structures on your layout? Of course not. You simply have to train yourself to look beyond the label on the box to find ways to make the kit look less like everyone else's model.

Sometimes a new coat of paint will help, but often more drastic measures are called for. Changing the use of a building to something other than what the kit maker intended is one way. You could take that hardware store kit, add a canopy, and put new signs on the front to turn it into a restaurant.

Or you could use the windows from a different kit to create a new look for a building. Better still, use a different kit to add some walls made from a different material to disguise the kit's origins with a minimum of effort.

Scratchbuilding

No other word strikes quite as much fear into the heart of many model railroaders. But there's no reason to be scared of scratchbuilding. Just think of it as a another very useful addition to your bag of model railroading tricks. In many ways it's easier than kitbashing, at least for me. The key to a successful scratchbuilding project is starting small and thinking in terms of what's included in a structure kit. Most kits include materials for walls, windows, doors, and roofs, and perhaps a photo of the finished model. The most important ingredient in a kit are the instructions. When you scratchbuild a model you have to round up the materials you need and then have to find or create the instructions. These can be as simple as a working sketch and published plan or a series of elaborate components.

An overwhelming selection of plastic and wood siding material is available. Also, a wide selection of door and window castings is offered by several manufacturers. And when planning your scratchbuilding project don't let the label on the package

Fig. 9-7 The only way I could get a model of the Essex Junction, Vermont, trainshed and station was to scratchbuild
it. The subwalls are styrene covered with Holgate & Reynolds HO scale brick, which is a bit oversized for N scale but
looks fine in person and in photos.

fool you. A sheet of HO scale brick can often be used as concrete block in N scale. Or 6-inch-wide HO clapboard material may provide those 12-inch-wide clapboards you need. Likewise, a small or medium HO scale window may be just what you need for a large N scale window for your project. Obviously, doors can't be adopted for different scales in the same manner.

In many cases scratchbuilding is the only way you can get that one perfect building for the layout that really sets the scene (fig. 9-7).

Specific scratchbuilding techniques are beyond the scope of this book, but you'll find helpful tips on scratchbuilding in almost every issue of *Model Railroader*. Just one piece of advice on scratchbuilding: start small. Don't attempt Grand Central Terminal as your first project. Start with a small, simple building—four walls and a roof—and get familiar with the process. As your confidence grows you'll be tackling bigger and more complex projects. And before you know it, you'll be wondering why anyone is scared of scratchbuilding.

PHOTOCOPYING TIP

Many right-of-way structures are available in N scale. If you would rather build your own, plans for many have appeared in *Model Railroader* magazine and other publications over the years. If you should find plans published in a scale larger than N, simply place the original drawing on a photocopier and reduce the drawing to N scale. For example, if using an HO scale original, set the copier to 52.5 percent to reduce the plan to N scale. This will give you a plan that can serve as a template for building the model. Most drawings published in model railroad magazines include a notice granting permission for readers to make such copies for their personal use.

CHAPTER TEN

MODULAR RAILROADING

What if you're interested in model railroading, but don't have the space, or time, for a large layout? Perhaps you want to find out if you really like the hobby, or you simply want to sample a little bit of every aspect of the hobby to find which part(s) you really like. Or maybe you want to spend more time with other model railroaders and spread the good word about how much fun model railroading is to others. All of these are good reasons to get involved in modular railroading.

The N scale version of modular railroading is called Ntrak. To become an Ntrakker (as the folks who participate in Ntrak call themselves) you simply have to build an Ntrak module. A module is a scene built on a module that is generally 2 feet wide and can be 4, 6, or 8 feet long. The newly developed oNetrak modules follow similar standards but use only a single line of track.

The key to modular railroading is that every module is built to the same set of standards so that it can be connected to any other module built to the same standards, anywhere in the world. Periodically model railroads get together and connect the modules together to create layouts much larger than any one modeler would ever be able to build and maintain. Some Ntrak layouts at the national conventions have measured more than 50 x 150 feet in size and have been made up of more than 300 individual modules.

Fig. 10-1 Bernie Kempinski used Walthers HO scale steel mill kits to create this looming N scale mill on his Ntrak modules. Bernard Kempinski

Fig. 10-2 *Model Railroader* managing editor Jim Kelly built this module based on Bena Siding, California, on the Southern Pacific near the famed Tehachapi Loop.

Modular standards have been established for all scales and gauges, but Ntrak was the first widespread modular railroad concept. And it remains the most popular today. The reasons are varied, but perhaps the most important is that in 1:160 proportion you can build an extensive and complete scene in that 2 x 4-foot standard module. You can build an industrial complex with lots of switching, a big bridge, or a mountain range that dwarfs the trains. If one module isn't enough to include everything you want, but you need to limit the size of each piece to 2 x 4 feet, build a 2 x 8-foot module that breaks into two for transport. In fact, the "module" can be divided into as many sections as necessary. As long as the tracks end up the right distance from the edge of the benchwork and don't exceed the minimum grade and curve standards, any length (in increments of 2 feet) is an Ntrak module.

Some Ntrakkers build modules based on several different prototypes. Others use the modules as their home layouts, perhaps with curved track sections that allow the layout to fit their space. Other modelers combine their efforts into an Ntrak club layout, where each member builds a layout to a common theme (members help each other out).

History

Ntrak began when Ben Davis, of Huntington Beach, California, thought it up in 1973. Ben belonged to the Belmont Shores Model Railroad Club, which has a large permanent layout. Ben wanted to figure out a way to show N scale to the model railroaders attending the 1974 convention in San Diego. With the help of some fellow club members, Ben built the first Ntrak module a year before the convention. Others followed and the modular layout, with its 50- to 100-car trains, was an immediate hit. The idea took off, and Ntrak modules were being built all over the country.

Ben coordinated the Ntrak effort and published the *Ntrak Newsletter* until 1977. Ben then stepped down and Jim FitzGerald took over as Ntrak coordinator. If you want to get started in Ntrak, but first want to find out if there is a club in your area, you can contact Ntrak by writing them at the address shown with the N scale suppliers and organizations listed in the back of this book.

Visibility

You could debate it, but many people feel the current popularity of N scale in particular, and model railroading in general, is due in large part

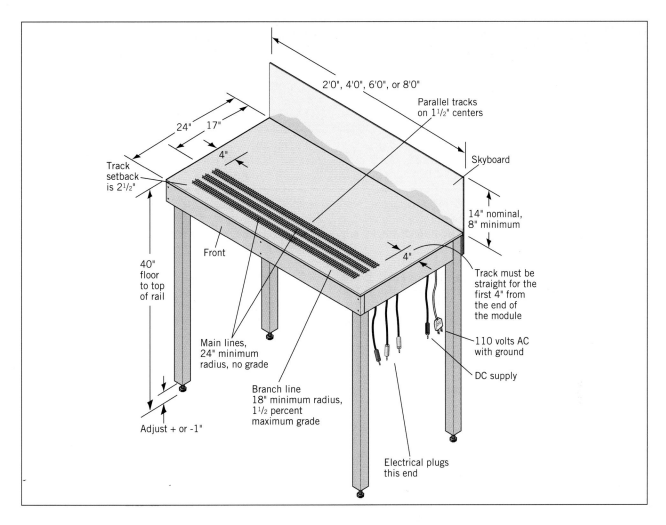

Parallel tracks
on 1½" centers

2'0", 4'0", 6'0", or 8'0"

24" 17"

4"

Skyboard

Track
setback
is 2½"

14" nominal,
8" minimum

Front

4"

40"
floor
to top
of rail

Track must be
straight for the
first 4" from
the end of the
module

110 volts AC
with ground

Main lines,
24" minimum
radius, no grade

DC supply

Branch line
18" minimum radius,
1½ percent
maximum grade

Adjust + or -1"

Electrical plugs
this end

Fig. 10-3 **Standard Ntrack module**

Fig. 10-4 **Another one of Bernie Kempinski's modular efforts—this time a oNetrak module based on the Canton District near Baltimore, Maryland.** Bernard Kempinski

Height of track: Rail tops 40" above floor

Basic module dimensions: Frame lengths in multiples of 1 foot. Twelve inches is the minimum width. This width may be increased up to 1 foot front or back for a total maximum width of 3 feet.

Module interface: C-clamps between modules. Track connections provided with one standard 4.91" Atlas straight section.

Track: Code 80 rail standard. Code 55 acceptable, provided code 80 transistors are used at module interface. One track is required, although additional tracks are permitted.

Minimum radius: 18" with appropriate easements.

Track location: On straight modules the location of the main has no real impact on the loop of modules and is not important, but generally the track is set back 4" to 6" from the nominal front so that the fascias may be reasonably aligned. Double or triple track should have 1W track center spacing at the module interface.

Corners: Corner modules are 30 x 30 inches, 3 x 3 feet, or 4 x 4 feet. Track should be set back 6" from the nominal front edge.

Electrical: Main line has red coded plug per Ntrak practices. The white and 110-volt requirements are the same as Ntrak. There are no special DCC wiring requirements. Use Ntrak standards for wire gauge.

For more information on oNetrak and a complete set of guidelines, send a self-addressed, stamped envelope and 25 cents to:

Ntrak
c/o Jim FitzGerald
1150 Wine Country Place
Templeton, CA 93465

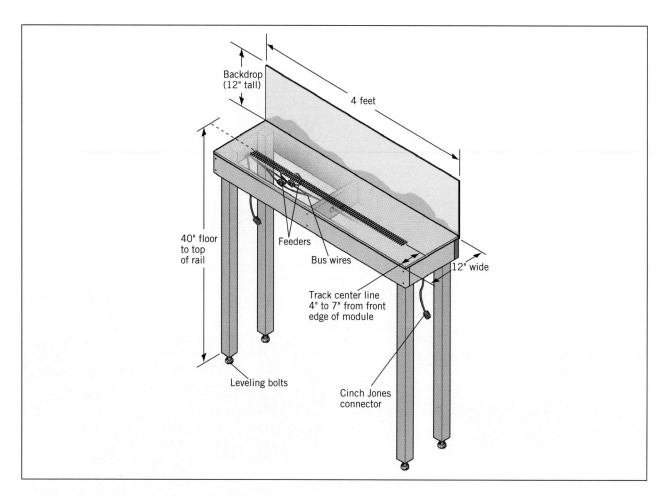

Fig. 10-5 Standard oNetrack module

to the efforts of the thousands of modelers involved in Ntrak. Before modular railroading took off, model railroading was a closed hobby. If you were interested in model trains, you had to seek out information and other modelers. You neighbor could be a model railroader and you would never know it until, and unless, you were invited into his house to see the layout.

And while model trains have always been popular during the holidays, store owners and train show promoters had to be content with small, stand-alone layouts as attractions. The development of Ntrak meant they could have large, operating, and portable displays that could be set up and taken down within a few hours. Shopping malls and Ntrak seem to go hand in hand, and mall managers, constantly on the lookout for ways of enticing shoppers to come out to the mall, find modular layouts irresistible. Ntrak clubs like the fact that the mall means lots of people see the trains (what's the point of modular railroading if no one sees your efforts?) and the space for setup is usually ideal, with wide aisle areas and good lighting. Some Ntrak clubs get space for setups provided free of charge, provided they run trains for a few hours while the stores are open.

Best of all, Ntrak brings the hobby of model railroading to a whole group of people. Men, women, and children who may have never heard of model railroading see an Ntrak layout, get hooked, and become model railroaders themselves. And the more model railroaders there are, the better is gets for all of us.

Modular standards

Figure 10-3 shows a standard Ntrak module. If you're planning to build a module I suggest obtaining a copy of the *Ntrak Manual*, which contains more detailed information and suggested track plans.

While Ntrak is now recognized as the *de facto* modular standard, Bernie Kempinski and some of his fellow modelers in the Northern Virginia Ntrak Club were becoming frustrated trying to design Ntrak modules based on prototype scenes. The limitations imposed by the three-track Ntrak arrangement led them to develop oNetrak, which, as the name implies, is basically a one-track module. A typical oNetrak module is shown in figs. 10-5 and 10-6. Again, for more detailed information I suggest contacting the national Ntrak organization.

A number of very realistic track arrangements are possible using the oNetrak layouts, and oNetrak modules can serve to extend one of the three routes in the standard Ntrak layout, adding to the popularity and versatility of both systems. Several oNetrak track plans are included here to get you

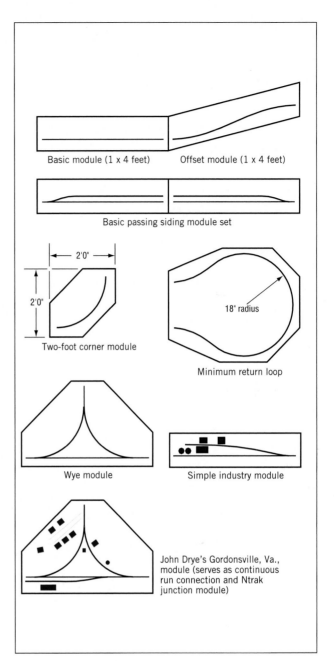

Fig. 10-6 oNetrak plans

started. And don't forget that modules built to either standard are great for use as a home layout. This is particularly appealing to apartment dwellers, students, and people in the military—in other words, anyone who moves fairly often. Simply take the layout with you and rearrange it as needed to fit into the basement or spare room in your next residence.

Whether you choose Ntrak or oNetrak, N scale modular railroading is a great way to enjoy the hobby. Building modules can become your sole hobby activity or can be an adjunct to home or club layout building.

CHAPTER ELEVEN

BUILD THE CAROLINA CENTRAL:1

An ordinary door and a theater trick are the heart of this layout you can build

There are many ways to learn about the hobby of model railroading, but the best (next to reading *Model Railroader*!) is by building a small layout. This project, the N scale Carolina Central, is a small subsidiary of the Southern Railway located somewhere near the Blue Ridge Mountains. We designed and built this layout with beginners in mind, but there's no reason it wouldn't keep a more experienced modeler entertained.

The track plan is the time-honored oval with an added twist. Hidden from view on the back side of the layout is a double-ended siding that serves as a staging track, so you can experiment with realistic operations. It gives the trains a place to go "beyond the layout." There's also a simple but challenging switching area located on the scenicked side of the layout. And if you ever get the bug, or space, to expand, the Seaboard Air Line interchange track would be an ideal place to start.

It's a brilliant spring day on the N scale Carolina Central, our latest project layout. We'll show you how we built it in the next two chapters.

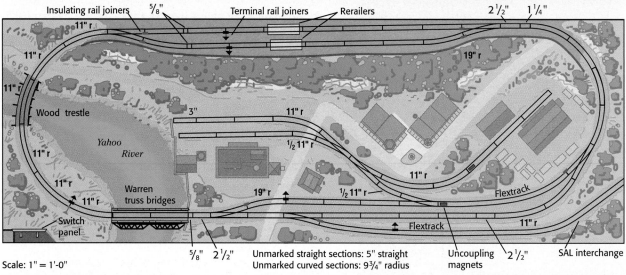

Insulating rail joiners   5/8"   Terminal rail joiners   Rerailers   2 1/2"   1 1/4"

11" r
11" r
11" r
19" r

Wood trestle
3"   11" r
1/2 11" r
Yahoo River
11" r
11" r   Warren truss bridges   19" r   1/2 11" r
11" r   Flextrack
Switch panel   11" r
Flextrack   11" r
SAL interchange
5/8"   2 1/2"   Uncoupling magnets   2 1/2"
Unmarked straight sections: 5" straight
Unmarked curved sections: 9 3/4" radius

Scale: 1" = 1'-0"

Fig. 11-1 Track Plan

BILL OF MATERIALS

Benchwork
28" x 80" interior door
1 x 4 lumber, 28" long (4)
folding table legs
1" electrical conduit, 20" long (4)
Styrofoam-compatible latex
  Liquid Nails
drywall screws
1" hardwood dowel, 18" long (4)
1" foam board, 4 x 8 sheet (1)
T nuts, bolts, and wing nuts (4 each)
sheet metal screws (8)

Atlas
2538 insulated joiners (1 pack)
2539 terminal joiners (3 pairs)
2546 Warren truss bridge (2)
92500 30" flextrack (3)
92501 5" straight (28)

92509 Snap Track assortment (2)
92510 9 3/4" radius curve (6)
92520 11" radius curve (9)
92521 1/2 11" radius curve (2)
92532 rerailer (2)
92702 standard left-hand turnout (4)
92703 standard right-hand turnout (4)

Blair Line Bridge Co*
67 timber trestle

Electrical
single-pole, single-throw
  switches (2)
single-pole, double-throw switch (1)
electrical junction box (1)

Midwest Products
3019 N scale cork roadbed (14)

Model Rectifier Corp.
2400 Railmaster power pack

S & L Enterprises**
totally hidden uncoupler (2)

Miscellaneous
push pins
wood carpenter's glue

* Blair Line Bridge Co.
P. O. Box 2291
Lee's Summit, MO 64063

** S & L Enterprises
5806 Miriam Dr.
Sykesville, MD 21784

A theme

Before getting down to the nuts and bolts of construction, let's consider the importance of a theme. The best model railroads all seem to have a well-defined one that gives the layout a sense of purpose and ties all the elements together.

Our theme is straightforward: The Carolina Central is a Southern Railway branch that connects with the Seaboard Air Line somewhere in the Carolina foothills. We wanted to capture the feel of this region using ready-to-run equipment and simple kits. A wide lazy river, a town square, and an old brick textile mill became key elements of our theme.

To increase the apparent size of the layout, we included the two backstage tracks. But the understated scenery found in this area meant that we had to come up with a simple but effective way of hiding the train once it went "backstage." A tunnel was out because they are scarce in the Carolina sandhills. A low tree-covered ridge did a remarkable job of hiding the staging tracks from view.

Start with a door

The foundation of the Carolina Central is a 26" x 80" interior hollow-core door. Check the "seconds" or "damaged" pile at the local lumberyard. Since you'll be covering the door with scenery, a few dings or bangs won't matter. Just make sure that the door is flat and the edges intact because they provide most of the structural strength.

We used folding table legs to support the door. These legs aren't necessary, but they make it much easier to build and operate the layout. The folding legs have an added advantage since they make the layout self-contained for transporting to shows. If moving the layout isn't a consideration, you can use bookshelves, sawhorses, or heavy cardboard boxes to raise the layout to a convenient height.

The folding table legs were a big improvement, but the layout was still too low for comfortable viewing, so we extended the legs with 1" electrical conduit to a more pleasing height. Leveling bolts inserted into the T nuts in the bottom of the legs make it easy to keep the Carolina Central on an even keel.

1 INSTALLING LEGS

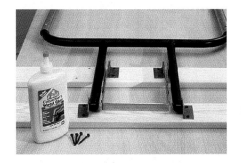

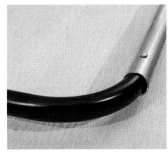

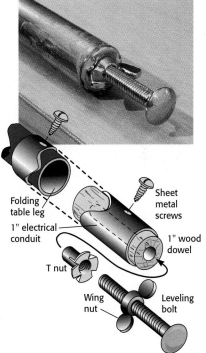

The position of the folding legs and braces determines the location of the 1 x 4 supports. Just be sure you attach the legs to the 1 x 4s, not the door. Cut four 1 x 4s 28" long and apply a bead of Liquid Nails. Place each 1 x 4 in position and secure it with drywall screws. Keep the screws about 1" from the edge, since the center of the door is hollow. our folding table legs weren't tall enough to suit us, so we slipped a 20"-long piece of 1" electrical conduit over each one. Then we secured the conduit to the legs with sheet metal screws. If you don't want to drill pilot holes into the conduit, you could use epoxy.

Folding table leg
1" electrical conduit
Sheet metal screws
1" wood dowel
T nut
Wing nut
Leveling bolt

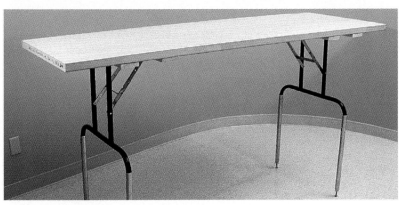

Flip the table over, adjust the height leveling bolts until everything is steady, and the completed table is ready for the next step.

To make the legs adjustable, we added T nuts to the bottom of each, hammering them into wood dowels as shown in the diagram. Don't worry if the dowel splits. In fact, it seems to lock the T nut in place more securely. Place a wing nut on the leveling bolt before screwing the bolt into the bottom of the leg. The wing nut will lock the bolt in place.

Any model railroad looks better when the scenery extends below the track. We used a piece of 1" foam board (get the pink or blue building insulation from a lumberyard, not the white beadboard material) and cut it to match the door. Mark the location of the river on the foam board. Feel free to make the river any size you'd like—just be sure the bridges can span it!

Lay the foam board on top of the door and position the sectional track and key structures. This track arrangement is close to the one we used, although we moved some structures around. Don't worry about the flextrack sections for now.

I used a utility knife to cut out the river and attached the foam board to the door with Styrofoam-compatible latex Liquid nails. An arrangement of C-clamps and heavy weights (in this case bound volumes of MR) held the foam while the Liquid Nails set.

Some additional details

We cemented a layer of 1" foam insulation board directly to the door. This makes it easy to add scenery below track level. Cork roadbed and Atlas track are easy to find and simple to work with, so we used them. Our control system is an MRC power pack mounted on a removable shelf. Three switches let us kill power to the passing siding, SAL interchange track, and either of the two storage tracks.

Time to get started!

This time around we'll concentrate on getting the Carolina Central up and running. We'll review the benchwork, tracklaying, and wiring. These skills aren't difficult, but they take time, practice, and patience to ensure satisfying results.

But nothing will get done if you just sit there! Let's stop all this jabbering and get started now. Don't y'all know there's an N scale railroad waiting to be built?

We used Midwest N scale cork roadbed. This material cuts down on the noise the trains make (although N scale trains are pretty quiet to begin with). More important, it makes the layout look more realistic since the track sits above the ground. We'll add some scale-size ballast after the track is down.

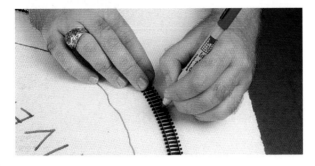

Reassemble the track directly onto the foam board. Don't try to force the pieces to fit if they won't—your only reward will be poor performance. If you have trouble getting the track to fit, double-check the pieces you're using because it's easy to get some pieces confused, especially the curved sections. Mark the center line of each piece of track with a pen. Once all the lines are drawn, remove the track.

Break the roadbed in half and spread some glue (we used Elmer's Carpenter's Glue) along the track center lines. Place one section of cork against the center line and secure it with push pins while the glue sets.

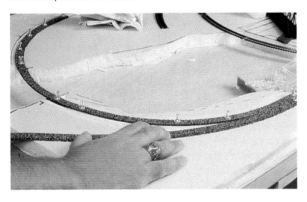

Place the second half of the cork snugly against the section that's already in place. Use push pins to hold the cork. I find it easier to run the cork across the river areas and trim it after the glue dries.

Installing the cork roadbed at a turnout is simple. Lay the cork in place through one route of the turnout just as you would for ordinary straight or curved track.

After the glue has dried, place the cork for the diverging route in position with a little overlap and cut through both layers of cork with a sharp hobby knife.

Repeat the process with the other half of the cork roadbed. Apply the glue and hold the pieces in place with push pins until everything has dried.

4 CREATING A "BACKSTAGE"

Painting the areas black you don't want people to look at is an old theater trick we used for the double-ended siding that serves as "everywhere else." To avoid getting paint on the track, we painted the cork and the foam board with black latex paint prior to tracklaying.

The black paint indicates these staging tracks are not part of the "real world."

5 INSTALLING BRIDGES

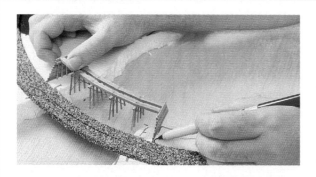

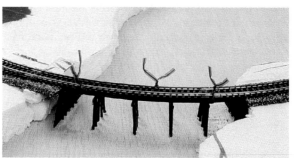

We used two Atlas through girder bridges near our textile mill, but Blair Line's curved wood trestle kit seemed a perfect addition to our Southern Railway branch. George Sebastian-Coleman assembled our trestle. Then I used it to determine how much foam board to remove. A sharp hobby knife made quick work of the cork roadbed and the excess foam board.

Before installing our trestle I gave it a wash with heavily diluted Polly Scale Engine Black. This made the wood look as if it had been treated with creosote. After the track had been laid, we used carpenter's glue to hold the trestle to the track. The twist ties are a simple way to keep the track against the trestle deck until the glue sets.

6 UNCOUPLING MAGNETS

Jeff Wilson and I equipped the rolling stock on the Carolina Central with Micro-Trains Magne-Matic couplers. These are operated from small magnets located between the rails or hidden under the ballast. We tried the rare earth magnets from S & L enterprises. They're simple to install and work great, even through the ballast.

Place the magnets in position on the metal plate according to the instructions. The location of our magnetic coupler is shown on the track plan. Cut a hole in the cork roadbed.

Apply a bead of carpenter's glue to the hole in the roadbed and drop the uncoupler into position. Once the track is installed and ballasted, the magnet is completely hidden from view.

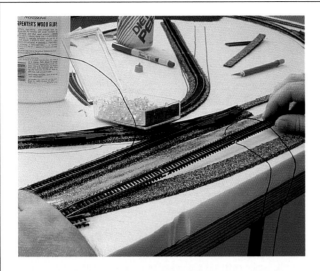

We reassembled our sectional track on the cork roadbed, then we added terminal rail joiners at the locations shown on the track plan. These come with a length of feeder wire soldered in place. We also added plastic insulated rail joiners where shown on the plan. These are important for wiring the layout, so make sure you get them in the right places.

Once the track fit properly, we ran a thin coat of Elmer's glue along the top of the cork roadbed and placed the track in position. This is the time to make any minor adjustments. The track was held in position with push pins until the glue hardened. The glue holds the track securely so there's no need to use track nails or spikes.

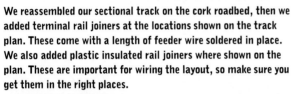

Flextrack comes in three-foot lengths and is the choice of most experienced modelers, since it produces smooth, flowing curves and frees you from the rigid geometry of sectional track. You will have to trim the flextrack to the proper length. Place a length of

track in position. One rail will extend longer than the other. Use a hobby knife to mark a notch on the long rail that's even with the end of the shorter rail. Use your hobby knife to trim away any ties that will interfere with the cut.

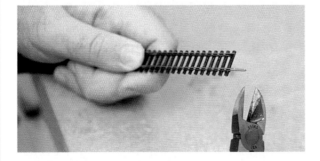

We cut the rail with special rail nippers. Use these for track and nothing else. Line up the nippers with the notch you marked and cut the rail to length. Wear safety goggles to protect your eyes from metal fragments.

File the bottom, top, and web of the cut rail smooth. Slip on a rail joiner and you're ready to install the flextrack on the layout. We secured the flextrack using the same glue and push pin technique we showed before.

Jim used an electrical box for our control panel. He drilled the underside to fit a ¾" piece of conduit, then drilled a hole through the door and connected the wires to the feeders. Insetting the box protects the switches from damage.

All the toggle switches are mounted in holes drilled in a plain switch cover. The power pack plugs into the outlet, making it easy to remove the power pack for storage.

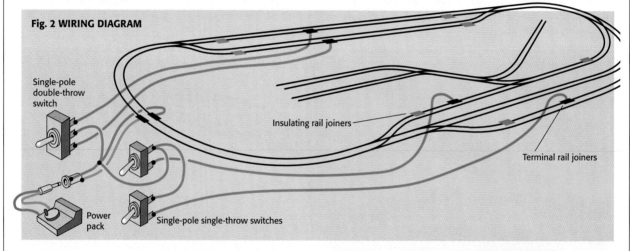

Fig. 2 WIRING DIAGRAM

Single-pole double-throw switch

Insulating rail joiners

Terminal rail joiners

Power pack

Single-pole single-throw switches

The Carolina Central's wiring is extremely simple, but it does what any layout's wiring should—it supports the railroad's operating scheme. You could easily add a pair of feeders to the track and be ready to roll, but adding several on/off tracks lets us hold engines backstage or on the interchange track. We also isolated the passing siding in the middle of town. That way the local can wait in the hole for the through freight. The illustration above shows how Jim Hediger wired the Carolina Central.

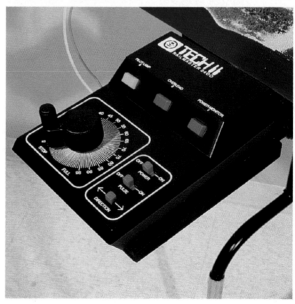

Our MRC power pack is mounted on a small shelf. Jim added a length of plywood across one set of the 1 x 4s that support the legs. A notch in one end of the plywood shelf makes it easy to slip the shelf in place.

Benchwork, track, and wiring are only the beginning. In the next chapter the Carolina Central comes to life as we add scenery, structures, and details.

All for now

Hook up the wires, plug in the power pack, and enjoy operating trains on the Carolina Central. This is a good time to make sure everything is working properly. Our locomotive is an Atlas GP9 that's an ideal choice for a small layout. The cars are from Micro-Trains, InterMountain, Atlas, and Walthers. We weathered all the rolling stock before placing it in service on the road.

Spend the next few weeks running trains, and don't worry that the landscape looks more like a pink desert than the Carolina foothills. We'll fix that in the next chapter, when we get together to create some scenery.

CHAPTER TWELVE

BUILD THE CAROLINA CENTRAL:2

Ballast, scenery, and structures finish off our N scale project layout

Now the trains are running and we're ready to make the Carolina Central look like part of the real world

Although every model railroader does things differently, the initial stages of layout construction—benchwork, track-laying, and wiring—leave little leeway for freedom of expression. It's a good idea to adhere to proven methods to make sure the trains run. But freedom of expression is what scenery is all about.

Most beginning model railroaders have the impression that scenery is beyond their abilities. Nothing could be further from the truth. Scenery is easy and a lot of fun. Use some commercial products and our step-by-step instructions and you'll be surprised at how good the finished product looks. For more tips on scenery, check out Dave Frary's book *How to Build Realistic Model Railroad Scenery,* published by Kalmbach Books.

In this chapter we'll bring the layout to life with scenery and details.

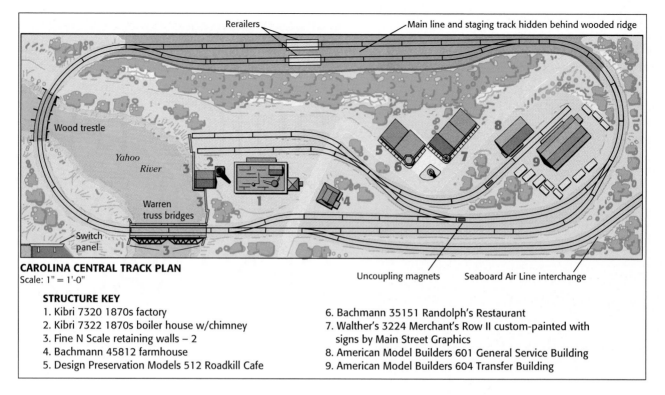

Rerailers

Main line and staging track hidden behind wooded ridge

Wood trestle

Yahoo River

Warren truss bridges

Switch panel

CAROLINA CENTRAL TRACK PLAN
Scale: 1" = 1'-0"

Uncoupling magnets   Seaboard Air Line interchange

STRUCTURE KEY
1. Kibri 7320 1870s factory
2. Kibri 7322 1870s boiler house w/chimney
3. Fine N Scale retaining walls – 2
4. Bachmann 45812 farmhouse
5. Design Preservation Models 512 Roadkill Cafe

6. Bachmann 35151 Randolph's Restaurant
7. Walther's 3224 Merchant's Row II custom-painted with signs by Main Street Graphics
8. American Model Builders 601 General Service Building
9. American Model Builders 604 Transfer Building

About the structures

The emphasis in this chapter is on scenery, so we're leaving the structures up to you and the instructions that come with the kits. The list above shows the structure kits we used. We tried to use only kits that fit in with our theme. At the same time we wanted to give you a variety of materials to work with, so the two major structure materials, wood and plastic, are represented.

Far more N scale structure kits are available than we could hope to include on our layout, so don't let our choices limit yours. Visit your hobby dealer and select the structures that appeal to you and suit your theme.

Two industries dominate the Carolina Central. The first is Burton Textiles. It's a Kibri plastic kit of a European prototype. It goes together in less than an evening, and with a little weathering it looks just like an eastern mill building.

Our second major industry, the G. S. C. Lumber Co., consists of two American Model Builders laser-cut wood kits. These require some care to assemble and will take two or three evenings, but the finished model is one you'll be proud to display for years to come.

At first glance these wood kits might not seem appropriate for beginners, but I was surprised to find the laser-cut structures are easier to build

than some of the plastic so-called beginner's kits on the market.

Our small downtown area features a Walthers Merchant's Row kit we borrowed from Main Street Graphics. This firm offers a line of window signs designed to fit specific kits, as well as a custom kit-building service. A finished sample of the Merchant's Row kit showed up for our new products department and we knew it was perfect for our town.

Be sure to plant all of your buildings in the ground. Nothing looks worse than a telltale gap where there should be a foundation. We placed all the structures on the layout, secured them with cement, and covered any remaining gaps with dirt or ground foam.

Get rolling

One last word of advice when it comes to adding scenery and details to your layout: take your time. There's no rush for you to finish, and once you get going new ideas seem to pop up all the time.

Just don't use a patient approach as an excuse to never get started. Go ahead and take the plunge. Scenery is easy and a lot of fun. Remember, even the absolutely worst scenery has to look better than that flat pink board.

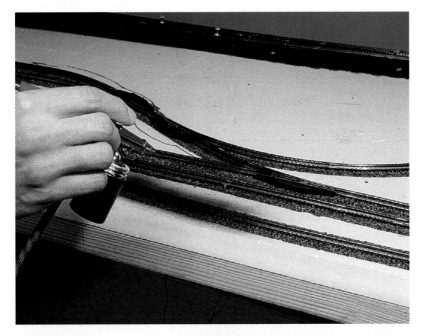

The silver rails and shiny plastic ties on our track didn't look realistic, so George Sebastian-Coleman airbrushed the track and rails with a mixture of Testor's Boxcar Red and Rail Brown before Jim Kelly arrived with the ballast.

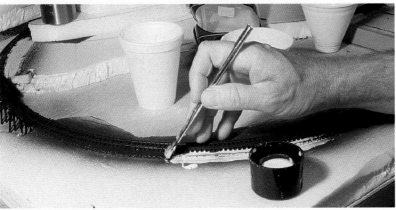

To avoid having a crusty top layer of ballast with loose granules underneath, Jim used an inexpensive brush to apply full-strength yellow glue to the sides of the cork roadbed. Don't put glue between the rails.

While the glue was still wet, Jim applied the initial layer of ballast. He used Woodland Scenics fine gray, but other brands will work just fine. A small plastic drinking cup is handy for sprinkling the ballast onto the tracks.

Next, Jim used a soft brush to shape the ballast and wipe away any excess material. Work carefully. You want to leave the surface of the ballast just below the tops of the ties. Make certain there are no loose grains of ballast on the sides of the rails or in the turnouts. They will cause operational problems later on.

Jim misted the ballast with "wet" water. That's water with a few drops of dishwashing detergent added. The detergent breaks the water's surface tension so it will more easily soak into the ballast. If you have trouble with the ballast flowing all over the place you can substitute rubbing alcohol for the water.

Once the ballast was thoroughly soaked, Jim dribbled a 50:50 mixture of diluted matte medium and water on the ballast, dripping some between each tie and along both sides of the roadbed. Don't try to ballast the entire railroad at once! You'll get tired, and that's when you'll make mistakes.

2 INSTALLING RETAINING WALLS

We used Fine N Scale retaining wall material for the retaining walls under the textile mill and the bridge abutments. Measure the retaining wall material in place and mark the cut line.

The resin material is easy to cut to size. Scribe along the line with a sharp hobby knife, using a metal straightedge to guide the blade. Then snap the pieces apart by bending along the scribed line.

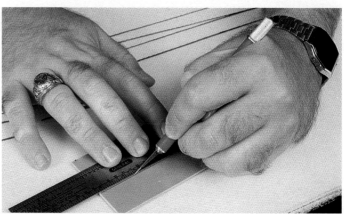

Angle the wall sections with sandpaper to avoid leaving any visible gaps at the corners. Then apply glue to the rear of the wall section.

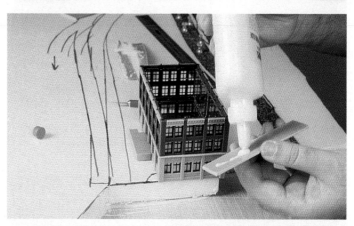

We used an assortment of metal weights and small pieces of wood to hold the wall sections in place while the glue sets.

3 SHAPING THE STYROFOAM

A low ridge holds the scenicked portion of our layout from the staging area. George made the ridge by stacking three narrow pieces of 1" foam on top of each other, attaching them to one another and the layout with latex Liquid Nails and weighting them overnight.

George used a hot wire cutter from the Foam Factory to shape our ridge. The wire heats up and literally melts its way through the foam.

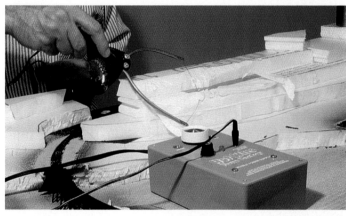

I used a wire wheel in a variable-speed power drill to shape the contours of the riverbanks. It's a quick but fairly messy way to carve the foam.

George mixed some Sculptamold to a putty-like consistency and liberally covered the hillsides and any visible joints between the foam board pieces. We like to use Sculptamold because it's lighter and more durable than plaster and takes longer to set, giving us more working time.

4 BASIC TEXTURING

I used a cheap brush to apply a thick coat of earth-colored latex paint to the hillsides. Be sure to cover the track and ballast with masking tape to protect them from splattering paint.

While the paint was wet, I sprinkled on various shades and textures of Woodland Scenics ground foam. A shaker jar really speeds this process along. Ours are food jars with holes punched in the lids.

5 ROCK OUTCROPPINGS

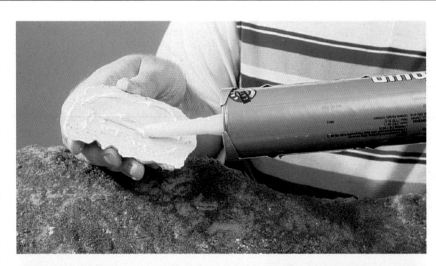

A few rock outcroppings provide some visual relief from the almost solid foliage we added to our ridge. The rocks are plaster castings made from Woodland Scenics rock molds. Once the plaster hardened, I removed the rock from the mold and cemented it on with Liquid Nails.

Drybrush the rocks to highlight the details. Apply a small amount of white paint to a scrap of cardstock and dip a stiff-bristled brush into the paint. Wipe most of the paint off the brush and lightly brush the little that's left over the raised areas of the rock casting.

I blended the castings into the hillside with Sculptamold. Then I added a few drops of India ink to a spray bottle of water and sprayed the rock surface. The ink will settle into the crevices, creating a very realistic effect. Repeat this process until the rocks look right.

I sketched out the path of the roads on the foam board and then used cork roadbed as a base for the roads, fastening it to the layout with carpenter's glue. The paved road is Evergreen .015" styrene sheet cut to 24 scale foot widths.

To make railroad crossings, use a hobby knife to trim the styrene to match track curvature. Trim it flush with the outside of the rails. Check the flange clearance with a car before adding styrene between the rails.

I scribed expansion joints in the street every 12 scale feet or so. I also used the knife to add cracks to the surface of the street. These aren't visible now, but they really stand out once the street is weathered.

Blend the shoulder of the road into the scenery with Sculptamold, then paint the road Badger Modelflex Concrete Gray.

I applied powered black and brown pastel chalks to the roads with a brush and used my fingers to create streaks down the center of each traffic lane.

7 DIRT ROADS AND LOTS

Dirt roads present a nice contrast to the paved ones. I made ours by applying a thin layer of Sculptamold to the cork. A putty knife works well for creating realistic ruts.

After painting the dirt roads and parking areas with our earth color I applied a layer of texture material, in this case Highball Earth. Sifted real dirt would also work.

I used a roll of masking tape to pack the texture dirt down. Do this while the paint is still wet, then mist the area with diluted matte medium to secure the dirt.

8 ADDING GROUND TEXTURE

Our initial layer of ground covering certainly looks much better than the plain foam board, but it's too smooth and regular. We placed additional texture throughout the foreground of the layout, but the hillside was textured as shown in step 10.

To create weed-grown areas I stretched out some Woodland Scenics poly fiber, misted it with matte medium, and sprinkled on some fine AMSI yellow and light green foam to represent wildflowers. Again, you want them growing in clumps here and there.

The Yahoo River is the scenic highlight of the Carolina Central. Once the bridge abutments were in place, George poured a soupy mixture of molding plaster to form the river bottom. Make a dam out of masking tape where the river runs off the layout. It's also a good idea to put a waterproof drop cloth below the layout to prevent disaster.

After the plaster set we painted the deepest areas of the river with flat black latex paint. To represent the shallower areas we feathered in earth-colored paint toward the banks and around the bridge piers and abutments. Keep the track covered with masking tape to protect it through the next step.

The water is Enviro-Tex, a two-part resin material that dries to a glossy surface. Follow the instructions for mixing and applying this material. The resin creeps up the banks as it cures. This can't be prevented, so after the resin hardened completely I blended the edges of the river with ground foam and texturing materials.

10 ADDING TREES

Even a small layout like ours would need hundreds of trees to simulate the look of eastern mountains in the late spring. Luckily all we needed were the tops of the trees. I used Woodland Scenics clump foliage (not the net foliage material) to cover the hillsides, first applying a liberal amount of Woodland Scenics Hob-E-Tac cement to the ground.

Stretch the foliage material apart in your fingers until it just starts to crumble, then apply it directly to the hillside. Don't push the material down; just let it lie naturally.

Since I used three different shades of green, the completed hill had a salt-and-pepper effect. A misting of matte medium and some medium green foam blended everything.

Melanie Buellesbach built all of our foreground trees from Woodland Scenics plastic armature tree kits. As she finished a batch of trees I misted them with matte medium and sprinkled on some fine green foam before installing them on the layout. We didn't keep track of how many trees there are, but I think we'll model a desert next time! Those trees aren't just for looks. They do an excellent job of screening the staging yard from view, eliminating the need for a tunnel portal.

11 FASCIA

Our fascia makes the layout more attractive. George and I placed the ⅛" Masonite against the side of the layout and marked the profile of the hills. Then he used a saber saw to cut it out and secured it to the side of the layout with Liquid Nails. Some green paint gave it a finished look.

The center of town is dominated by this statue of the local war hero. He's an **HO** **P**reiser band leader mounted on a styrene base.

Just the beginning

You can spend months or years adding details to even a small railroad like this. Since we didn't have years to devote to this project, we gave the layout what I call a "first coat" of detailing. We added enough signs, people, vehicles, and structures to create the appearance of a finished railroad.

But there's lots more that could be added. A backyard barbecue, a sign in the town square announcing an upcoming county fair, telegraph poles spaced along the track, small outbuildings, a scale house for the team track, and a couple of boats on the river would all make interesting projects. Flip through the Walthers N scale catalog, or better yet visit your hobby shop, and look at the variety of detailing parts available. Let your imagination—and your theme—be your guide. Good luck and, above all, have fun!

AAR: Association of American Railroads, the trade association that represents the common interests of the railroad industry in such areas as standards, public relations, and advertising.

ACI: Automatic car identification; see Kar Trak.

Articulated: A steam locomotive with two engines (i.e., cylinders, rods, and wheels) under one boiler.

Bad order: Defective, out of order.

Big hole: An emergency stop.

Big hook: Wrecking crane.

Boomer: An experienced railroad man who moves from railroad to railroad.

Block: A section of track.

Block signal: A signal at the entrance to a block indicating whether the block is occupied by a train.

Bolster: The crosswise member of the frame of a car at the truck (body bolster) or the crosswise piece at the center of a truck (truck bolster).

Branch line: Secondary line of a railroad.

Brass (also brass hat, brass collar): Railroad executives and officials.

Cab-forward: An articulated steam locomotive peculiar to the Southern Pacific, built with the cab in front for visibility in tunnels and snowsheds.

Caboose: The car that carries the crew of a freight train. It's almost always at the rear of the train. Slang terms for the caboose include buggy, bouncer, bobber, cabin, cage, crummy, hack, palace, and way car.

Camelback: A type of steam locomotive with the cab astride the boiler. The Camelback was a solution to the problem of forward visibility past the wide firebox required for burning anthracite.

Catenary: Overhead trolley wire system for locomotives and cars that use pantographs for current collection.

Class I railroad: A railroad with 5 million dollars or more in annual operating revenues. Class II railroads have revenues less than 5 million dollars per year. The third classification is Switching and Terminal Railroads.

Classification lights: Lights on the front of the locomotive that indicate the type of train. White lights show that the train is an extra, and green indicates that another section of the train is following.

Clear board: Green or proceed signal.

Climax: A type of geared steam locomotive used primarily by logging railroads. The two cylinders drive a jackshaft parallel with the axles. Power is transmitted to each truck through bevel gears and a driveshaft; rods couple the axles on each truck. See also Shay and Heisler.

Coaling station: A structure for storing coal and transferring it into locomotive tenders.

Consist: The cars which make up a train; also a list of those cars.

Continuous rail (also welded rail, ribbonrail): Rails which have been welded together to form a single rail hundreds of feet long, eliminating most rail joints, which are the weakest part of the track.

Cornfield meet: A meet out in the cornfields away from the station and the passing siding-i.e., a head-on collision.

Covered wagon: A diesel cab unit, A or B, as opposed to a hood unit.

Cowl unit: A diesel unit that looks like a cab unit but differs structurally in that the carbody is merely a fullwidth hood rather than a structural part of the unit.

Crossing: A track arrangement that permits two tracks to cross but does not allow trains to move from one track to the other.

Crossover: Two turnouts arranged back-to-back to allow trains to move from one track to another.

CTC: Centralized Traffic Control, the direct control of all turnouts and signals on a stretch of railroad by a single dispatcher.

Cut: Roadbed below the level of the surrounding terrain.

Cut of cars: A number of cars coupled together. The addition of marker lamps makes the cut of cars a train.

Deadhead: A car or train, usually passenger, moving empty; a passenger traveling on a pass. Empty freight cars are referred to as empties.

Decal: A type of lettering material for models. The letters and number, are printed on specially prepared pa - per and then coated with varnish. The lettering is applied by soaking the decal in water to dissolve the film between the ink and the paper, and placing the layer of varnish and ink on the car.

Derail: A device placed over the rail to prevent a car from rolling from a siding, for example, onto a main line.

Division: A portion of a railroad considered as an operational and administrative unit.

Doubleheader: A train pulled by two locomotives, each with an engine crew, as opposed to diesel or electric locomotive units operating in multiple as a single locomotive with one crew.

Doubling a hill: Splitting a train and taking it up a steep grade in two parts, one at a time.

Draft gear: The mechanism which connects the coupler to the frame of the car. In the model world, the coupler mounting box is sometimes called the draft gear.

Drawbar: Any coupling, either a solid bar or couplers, between two pieces of rolling stock.

Dry transfer: A lettering process in which the letter itself is a thin plastic film with a pressure-sensitive wax adhesive.

Enginehouse: A building in which locomotives are serviced.

Extra: A train not authorized by a timetable schedule.

Fill: Roadbed built up above the surrounding terrain.

Flange: The part of the wheel which runs below and inside the top of the rails to guide the wheel.

Gandy dancer: A track worker.

Gas-electric: A self-propelled car powered by a gasoline engine driving a generator which supplies current to motors on the axles. Gas-electrics were the common form of branchline passenger train in the 1920s and 1930s.

Glad hand: The metal coupling on the end of an air hose.

Grab iron: Handholds on the sides, ends, and roofs of cars.

Head-end cars: Mail, baggage, and express cars, usually run at the front of a passenger train.

Heisler: A type of geared steam locomotive used by logging railroads. It had two cylinders arranged in a V connected to a driveshaft which in turn was connected to the trucks. See also Climax and Shay.

Highball: A proceed signal.

Hood unit: A road-switcher, so called because of the construction of the locomotive, with the machinery covered by a hood rather than a full-width cab.

Hy-cube: A modern type of boxcar that is taller than standard and thus has a higher cubic capacity.

Helper: A locomotive added to a train to help it climb a grade.

High iron: The main line.

Hog: A locomotive.

Hogger: An engineer.

Hostler: A workman who services locomotives between runs.

Hotbox: An axle bearing that has become hot because of lack of lubrication.

Interchange: A junction of two railroads where cars are transferred from one line to the other.

Interlocking: A mechanical or electrical system of signaling that ensures that only one train at a time is allowed to move through a junction.

ICC: The Interstate Commerce Commission, an agency of the Federal government that regulated most forms of surface transportation. Among its powers were the approval of both instituting and discontinuing railroad service.

Interurban: An electrically operated light railway between cities and towns, as opposed to local streetcar service.

In the hole: In a siding to meet or pass another train.

Johnson bar: The manual reversing lever of older steam locomotives.

Journal: The load-bearing part of an axle. The weight of the axle is carried by the journal bearing, which is enclosed by the journal box.

Kar Trak: A modern system used to keep track of all railroad equipment. It employs ACI (automatic car identification) reflective labels on all rolling stock, trackside scanners, and computers.

Kingpin: The pivot on which a truck swivels. Center pin is the more common term for the prototype.

Kitbash: To combine parts from kits to produce a model unlike the straight kit models.

LCL: Less than Carload Lot, any shipment of freight too small to fill an entire car.

Main line: Any of the principal, heavy-traffic lines of a railroad.

Maintenance-of-way equipment: The machinery and rolling stock used to keep track and roadbed in good condition.

Markers: Lamps hung on the rear of the last car of the train to show that the cars are indeed a train and to indicate its status. Often nowadays substitutes are used, such as reflectors or a red flag jammed into the coupler. Similar lamps on the front of the locomotive are called classification lamps.

M.U.: Multiple unit, a method of controlling several diesel units, electric cars, or locomotives from one cab. M.U. cars are electric passenger cars for operation on electrified portions of a steam or diesel railroad, as in a suburban district. Interurbans, subway cars, and RDCs are technically M.U. cars, but the term is reserved for steam-road electric cars.

Muzzle-loader: A hand-fired steam engine, i.e., one without a mechanical stoker.

Narrow gauge: Track with a gauge less than 4 feet 8½ inches.

On the advertised: On time.

Pantograph: A current pickup device resembling a folding clotheshorse for electric locomotives and cars.

Piggyback: The movement of truck trailers on flat cars. Also called TOFC.

Pullman: A sleeping car or parlor car operated by the Pullman Company.

Pull the pin: Operate the uncoupling lever.

Rail Diesel Car (RDC): A self-propelled diesel-powered passenger car built by the Budd Company.

Railfan: A person who enjoys riding, watching, photographing, and reading about trains.

Reefer: A refrigerator car.

Red board: A signal indicating stop.

Right of way: The track, roadbed, and property along the track owned by the railroad.

Rip track: The track in a yard where minor car repairs are done.

Road-switcher: A general-purpose diesel that can be used for both yard switching and road duties. They are also called hood units.

Roundhouse: An enginehouse like a sector of a circle in shape, and usually surrounding a turntable.

Runaround: A switching maneuver in which the locomotive uncouples from its train, pulls ahead, backs past on an adjacent track, and moves forward to couple onto the rear of the train; also the track itself where the move takes place.

Saw-by: A maneuver by which two trains can meet at a siding which is too short to hold either.

Schedule: That portion of a timetable that lists the class, direction, number, and movement of regular trains.

Shay: A type of geared steam locomotive used extensively in logging. It had three cylinders mounted vertically on the right side of the boiler driving a crankshaft geared to all the axles.

Shoo-fly: A temporary track laid around an obstruction.

Short line: A small railroad, generally Class II.

Slip switch: A piece of trackwork that combines a crossing and four turnouts to permit trains to move from one track to the other or to simply stay on the same track.

Slug: A weighted locomotive unit with traction motors but no diesel engine or generator. It is used in conjunction with a diesel locomotive for additional tractive force.

Smokejack: A chimney on a car or building.

Snowshed: A structure built over the track in mountainous areas to protect the tracks from snow.

Spot a car: To place a car in its designated position, as at an industry or on a station track.

Spring switch: A turnout held in one position by a spring so that facing-point traffic always takes the same route but trailing-point traffic can run through the turnout from either track.

Superelevation: The raising of the outer rail on a curve; banking.

Talgo: A type of lightweight passenger train built by American Car & Foundry. In the model world the term is applied to truck-mounted couplers.

Tangent: Straight track.

Tank engine: A steam locomotive that carries its fuel and water supply in tanks hung over or alongside the boiler or on a frame extension at the rear instead of in a tender.

Tender: A car, attached to a steam locomotive, that carries extra fuel and water for the locomotive.

Throttle: The speed control of the locomotive; in the model world, a rheostat, variable transformer, or other speed controller.

Timetable: The authority for the movement of regular trains subject to the railroad's operating rules.

Ton-mile: One ton of freight moved one mile.

Traction: Public utility transportation; by extension, all electrically operated trains.

Transition curve: A section of track with a gradually diminishing radius between the straight track and the circular part of the curve. Also called a spiral.

Turnout: Track switch.

Turntable: A rotating bridge used for turning locomotives.

Unit: A diesel locomotive unit.

Unit train: A freight train that carries a single commodity from source to destination and returns empty.

USRA: United States Railroad Administration. The USRA was responsible for the operation of the country's railroads during World War I.

Varnish: A passenger train. Wooden passenger cars used to be given many coats of varnish.

Vestibule: The enclosed area at the end of a passenger car where the side doors are located. Early passenger cars had only an open platform. Around the 1890s narrow-vestibule cars came into use, with a vestibule only as wide as the passageway between the cars. The full-width vestibule followed soon after.

Water column: A standpipe adjacent to the track and connected to a water supply for filling steam locomotive tenders.

Wye: A track configuration for turning a locomotive or a train or for joining a branch to a main line for operation in both directions.

Yard engine (also yard goat): A switching locomotive.

American Limited Models
P. O. Box 7803
Fremont, CA 94537-7803

American Model Builders
1420 Hanley Industrial Ct.
St. Louis, MO 63144

Athabasca Scale Models Ltd.
771 Wilkinson Way
Saskatoon, SK Canada
S7N 3L8

Atlas Model Railroad Co.
378 Florence Ave.
Hillside, NJ 07205
www.atlasrr.com

Aztec Mfg. Co.
2701 Conestoga Ave., Unit 113
Carson City, NV 89706

Blair Line
P. O. Box 1136
Carthage, MO 64836-1136
www.blairline.com

Centerline Products
18409 Harmony Rd.
Marengo, IL 60152

Digitrax
450 Cemetary St., Suite 206
Norcross, GA 30071-4228

F&H Enterprises
2562 Silver State Parkway,
   Building C, Suite 3
Minden, NV 89423

Fine N Scale Products
4202 Blue Heron Cir.
Anacortes, WA 98221

GHQ
28100 Woodside Rd.
Shorewood, MN 55331
www.ghqmodels.com

Gold Medal Models
R.R.2 Box 3104
Lopez, WA 98261,

Hot Wire Foam Factory
300 N. G St.,
Lompoc, CA 93436

InterMountain Railway Co.
P. O. Box 839
Longmont, CO 80502-0839

Kato U. S. A.
100 Remington Rd.
Schaumburg, IL 60173

Life-Like Products Inc.
1600 Union Ave.
Baltimore, MD 21211

Micro-Trains Line
P. O. Box 1200
Talent, OR 97540-1200

Model Die Casting
5070 Sigstrom Ave.
Carson City, NV 89701

The N Scale Architect
3 Oxford Lane
Hackettstown, NJ 07840

Peco Railway Models
Pritchard Patent Product Co. Ltd.
Beer, Seaton, Devon, England
EX12 3NA

Rail Systems
510 S. E. Hamilton Ct.
Blue Springs, MO 64014

Red Caboose
P. O. Box 250
Mead, CO 80542

S&L Enterprises
5806 Miriam Dr.
Sykesville, MD 21784

Scenic Express
1001 Lowry Ave.
Jeannette, PA 15644

Showcase Miniatures
P. O. Box 753-N
Cherry Valley, CA 92223

Sylvan Scale Models
R. R. 2
Parkhill, Ontario, Canada
N0M 2K0

Wm. K. Walthers
P. O. Box 3039
Milwaukee, WI 53201-3039

Wangrow Electronics
1500 W. Laverne Ave.
 Park Ridge, IL 60068-2562

Woodland Scenics
P. O. Box 98
101 E. Valley Dr.
Linn Creek, MO 65052

X-acto (Division of Hunt Mfg.)
One Commerce Square
2005 Market St.
Philadelphia, PA 19103-7085

Xuron Corp.
60 Industrial Park Rd.
Saco, ME 04072